POEMS OF KANEKO MISUZU

AND

HAIKUS INSPIRED BY THEM I:

THE HEAVENS AND THE EARTH

MAYUMI ITOH

Copyright © Mayumi Itoh 2019
ISBN: 9781081558680

This work is subject to copyright. All rights are exclusively reserved by this author, including rights of reprinting, reuse of illustrations, translation, broadcasting and recitation, and reproduction in any form.

Cover design © Mayumi Itoh 2019
Front cover photograph: Entrance of Kaneko Misuzu Memorial Museum, Senzaki, Nagato, Yamaguchi prefecture, August 2012, taken by © Meg Itoh.
Back cover photograph: Portulaca blossoms (*hana suberihiyu, portulaca oleracea L. x P. pilosa L. subsp. grandiflora*), at the entrance of Kaneko Misuzu Memorial Museum, Senzaki, Nagato, Yamaguchi prefecture, August 2012, taken by © Meg Itoh.

In memory of

Donald Keene

who pioneered Japanese literature studies

and inspired countless students

Contents

List of Photographs..vi

Notes on the Text..viii

Acknowledgments..ix

Introduction...2

Chapter 1   January...7

Chapter 2   February..33

Chapter 3   March..59

Chapter 4   April...85

Chapter 5   May..107

Chapter 6   June...129

Chapter 7   July..155

Chapter 8   August...181

Chapter 9   September..207

Chapter 10	October	229
Chapter 11	November	253
Chapter 12	December	275

Notes...297

Selected Bibliography..............................306

About the Author...................................309

List of Photographs

All photographs were taken by the author, except for those credited below.

Photograph 1. Wooden plaque of Misuzu's poem entitled, "O-butsudan" (The Buddha's Altar), above the entrance door of a residence on Misuzu street, Senzaki, Nagato, Yamaguchi prefecture, August 2012, © Meg Itoh.

Photograph 2. Senzaki seen from Mt. Ōji, Ōmi Island, Nagato, Yamaguchi prefecture, August 2012, © Meg Itoh.

Photograph 3. Full moon in the spring.

Photograph 4. Coneflower with bees.

Photograph 5. Crescent moon.

Photograph 6. Rainbow.

Photograph 7. Sea and sky, Ōmi Island, Nagato, Yamaguchi prefecture, August 2012, © Meg Itoh.

Photograph 8. Goldfish.

Photograph 9. Tray with the design of a rabbit in the moon.

Photograph 10. Full moon with Mars (above the moon).

Photograph 11. Dandelion puff ball.

Photograph 12. Kadomatsu decoration for the new year, under Creative Commons license, "Pair gate with [bamboo and] pine branches for the new year, kadomatsu, Katori-city, Japan," January 2, 2007, https://commons.wikimedia.org/wiki/File:Pair_gate_with_pine_branches_for_the_New_Year,kadomatsu,katori-city,japan.JPG.

Notes on the Text

Names of Japanese persons are given with the surname first, except for those who use the reversed order in English. Honorific prefixes, such as doctor and mister, are not used in the text, except in direct quotations.

For romanization of Japanese, the Hepburn is primarily used, with macrons. However, macrons are not used for words known in English without macrons, as for Kyoto and Tokyo. Another exception is that "n" is not converted to "m" for words where it precedes "b, m, and p." Examples include tonbo (dragonfly), instead of tombo; sanma (Pacific saury), instead of samma; and tanpopo (dandelion), instead of tampopo.

All translations, including those of the poems of Kaneko Misuzu and the haikus of this author, were made by the author in the form of paraphrases (not as literal translations) for the sake of facilitating understanding.

Acknowledgments

For translating into English Kaneko Misuzu's poems from the original Japanese, *Kaneko Misuzu zenshū* (Complete Works of Kaneko Misuzu), Tokyo: JULA shuppan-kyoku, Vol. 1–Vol. 3 (1984) was primarily used, and the source for each poem is cited in the Notes at the end of this book. I would like to thank Kaneko Misuzu Memorial Museum Director Yazaki Setsuo and JULA Publisher Ōmura Yūko, for valuable documents and information, Meg Itoh, for the use of photographs, as well as the Hoshi no shima kukai (formerly the Haiku Society of New York), Tsuneo Akaha, Kent Calder, Toshiko Calder, Morrell Chance, Steve Clemons, Akiko Collcutt, Gerald Curtis, Martin Heijdra, Ronald Hrebenar, Imai Sanae, Itō Yayoi, Kumi Kato, Stephen Roddy, Watanabe Miyuki, and Vicki Wong, for encouragement and inspirations. I extend my appreciation to Gregory Rewoldt and Meg Itoh, for continuous support.

Kaneko Misuzu (April 1903–March 1930), Kaneko Misuzu Memorial Museum (former bookstore/residence of Kaneko Misuzu), Senzaki, Nagato, Yamaguchi prefecture, August 2012, taken by © Meg Itoh.

Introduction

This is a unique anthology of the first comprehensive English translations of poems of a Japanese female poet, Kaneko Misuzu (April 11, 1903–March 10, 1930; "Misuzu" hereafter), and also original haikus by this author, inspired by Misuzu's poems. Out of 512 poems Misuzu wrote, this work—volume one of four—includes 130 poems that embrace three major themes of haiku: 1) the seasons and the weather; 2) astronomy or the heavens; and 3) geography or the earth.

    Misuzu (her penname; her real name was Kaneko Teru) was born and grew up in the fishing village of Senzaki, Ōtsu, in current Nagato, on the northern coast of Yamaguchi prefecture, which is located on the western edge of Japan's main island, Honshū. Senzaki is a major seaport in the region, and the locale is surrounded by a pristine sea with stunning rock formations, presenting breathtaking views. These natural scenes have been preserved today, and the area is one of the nationally-designated parks.

Misuzu spent her childhood as a lonely girl. When she was two years old, her father died in Yingkou, a port city on the Liaodong peninsula, in northeastern China, where he worked as a bookstore manager. Afterward, her mother opened a bookstore in Senzaki and worked all day long, with her grandmother. After graduating from the local Ōtsu Higher Women's School, Misuzu moved in April 1923 to Shimonoseki, a major city of Yamaguchi prefecture on the southwestern coast, where her mother had married her uncle and helped his bookstore business. There, Misuzu began working at one of the branch bookstores of her uncle and began sending her poems to literary magazines. The rest is history.

Misuzu appeared like a comet in September 1923, at the zenith of a liberal poetry movement in Japan and was recognized as a giant rising star in poetry circles. She wrote more than 512 poems over six and a half years. Her poems, which she compiled into a three-volume anthology, are characterized by innocence, purity, sensitivity, and vivid imagination. They demonstrate profound empathy for all living things. Her sharp insight into nature and the universe did not overlook the smallest and weakest things on earth and in the heavens. Many of her soul-searching poems evoke the works of such female poets as Emily Dickinson and Christina Rossetti.

In turn, her personal life was overshadowed by a series of unsettling events, including the untimely death of her father, the adoption of her younger brother by her uncle (a family secret), who owned bookstores in Shimonoseki and in China, and then her mother's marriage to this uncle. This was followed by an arranged marriage of her own in February 1926 to a delinquent employee of her uncle. Her husband kept going to brothels and gave her gonorrhea (a sexually transmitted disease). She became gravely ill and sought a divorce, but her husband refused to grant her custody of their three-year old daughter. In March 1930, Misuzu suddenly ended her life at age 26 by taking a fatal dose of sleeping pills (For details of her life, see *Kaneko Misuzu: Life and Poems of A Lonely Princess*, 2018).

This anthology introduces Misuzu's poems entirely for the first time in English and also presents original haikus inspired by her poems. This is a homage to Misuzu's poems and to the poet herself and explores the deep and delicate inner world of Misuzu, who referred to herself as a "lonely princess."

Format of the Text

Out of 512 poems Misuzu wrote, this work includes 130 poems that pertain to the themes of the heavens and the earth and categorized them according to the twelve months and the four seasons (plus the "new year" which constitutes an independent 'season' because of its importance to Japanese culture). The text is formatted so that it presents one poem of Misuzu first on the left-hand page, and then one haiku inspired by this particular poem on the right-hand page.

Many of her original poems in Japanese use ambiguous expressions and the local dialect that even most Japanese do not understand. They also refer to things that do not exist in the Western world. In order to enhance understanding, Misuzu's poems are given in paraphrased translations and some annotations are added in brackets [ ], where the meaning was unclear in the English translation.

Each haiku is given in the original Japanese, along with its romanization, as well as its English translation. This is followed by the season word, an essential element in haiku, and the brief cultural and historical background for the poem and the haiku where applicable. This completes the entry for one poem and one haiku. Enjoy!

January

Photograph 1. Wooden plaque of Misuzu's poem entitled, "O-butsudan" (The Buddha's Altar), above the entrance door of a residence on Misuzu street, Senzaki, Nagato, Yamaguchi prefecture, August 2012, © Meg Itoh.

Yume uri (The Dream Seller)

At the beginning of the year

a dream seller

comes to sell

good first dreams.

His treasure boat

is like a mountain

loaded with

good first dreams.

The kind dream seller

also goes to the back alley

and quietly leaves

good first dreams,

for the lonely children

who cannot buy them.[1]

夢売りや

　　みすゞの初夢

　　　　叶えむと

Yume uri ya

　　Misuzu no hatsu yume

　　　　kanaen to

The dream seller

　　vowed to make Misuzu's first dream

　　　　on New Year's Day come true

Season word: *hatsu yume* (the first dream on the night of New Year's Day; signifies the new year)
"Hatsu yume" is believed to foretell the luck of a person for that year. Misuzu did not forget the underprivileged children even on the night of New Year's Day.

Yama ikutsu (How Many Mountains)

Behind the town
there is a low mountain.

Beyond the mountain
there is a village.

Beyond the village
there is a high mountain.

I do not know
what is beyond that.

I wonder
how many mountains
I should cross,

to see the golden castle
that I saw in a dream
in the past.[2]

初夢や

　　みすゞの願ひ

　　　　天翔ける

Hatsu yume ya

　　Misuzu no negai

　　　　ten kakeru

The first dream of New Year's Day

　　Misuzu's wish

　　　　gallops to heaven

Season word: *hatsu yume* (the first dream on the night of New Year's Day; new year)
"Hatsu yume" refers to the first dream on the night of New Year's Day, which in Japanese culture is believed to foretell the luck of a person for that year.

O-butsudan (The Buddha's Altar)

The daidai oranges I picked at the backdoor

and the flower-shaped sweets,

the souvenir from the town,

we cannot eat them

unless we offer them to Buddha first.

But Buddha is kind

and gives them to us soon,

so I hold my hands together politely

in appreciation to Buddha

before eating them.

There is no garden at our house,

but in the Buddha's alter,

there are always pretty flowers,

so our house is bright all over.

Buddha is kind

and gives me the flowers,

but I should not step

on the fallen flower petals.

Every morning and evening,

my grandmother lights the candle

in the Buddha's altar.

Inside the altar is all gold,

so it shines like a palace.

Every morning and evening,

I offer my appreciation

to Buddha without fail.

Then I remember the things

I have forgotten all day.

Even if I have forgotten about them,

Buddha always watches over me.

Therefore, I say

"Thank you, thank you, Buddha."

It looks like a golden palace,

but the gate is small.

If I were always a good child,

I could pass through the gate someday.[3]

Misuzu found her salvation in the enlightenment of Buddha. Most Japanese houses have a Buddha's altar in the guest room and make offerings to Buddha. Twice a day, they offer prayers for Buddha and their ancestors, whose souls are believed to rest in peace in the Pure Land of Paradise of Buddha.

橙飾る

　　御仏壇と

　　　　神棚と

Daidai kazaru

　　o butsudan to

　　　　kami dana to

Decorating the daidai oranges

　　on the Buddha's altar

　　　　and on the in-house Shinto shrine

Season word: *daidai kazaru* (to decorate *daidai* oranges as an offering for the Shinto gods for the new year; new year) It is a Japanese tradition to decorate *daidai* (bitter orange) on top of a layer of round rice cakes, as an offering for the Shinto gods for the new year, while most Japanese believe in Buddhism and make offerings to the Buddha's altar at home year around.

Asa to yoru (The Morning and the Night)

Where does the morning come from?

Peeking a little from the mountain in the east,
it gallops through the sky quickly
and descends on the town quietly.

It will not peek at such places,
as under the tree shade or under the floor
until the morning sun shines.

Where does the night come from?

Swelling up from under the floor
and from the tree shade,
it stands up tall under the eaves suddenly.

It will not reach
the end of the clouds
even if the sunset has gone.[4]

初日の出

　　朝の光に

　　　　夜見る娘

Hatsu hinode

　　asa no hikari ni

　　　　yoru miru ko

Sunrise on New Year's Day

　　the girl is looking at night

　　　　in the morning light

Season word: *hatsu hinode* (sunrise on New Year's Day; new year)

Kyonen (Last Year)

I saw a boat, I saw a boat
on New Year's Day,
on the first day of this new year,
a boat leaving this port
with a black sail and without a flag.

The boat, that boat,
who is riding on the boat?
Is it the old year, last year
that was chased out
by the first sunrise today? I see.

The boat is sailing, the boat is sailing.
Beyond where it is sailing,
is there a port where last year can land?
Is there someone who is waiting for last year?

I saw last year, I saw last year
on New Year's Day,
on the first day of this new year,
a shadow running away
to the west and further west,
riding on the boat with a black sail.[5]

去年今年

　　黒き帆去りて

　　　　白帆来る

Kozo kotoshi

　　kuroki ho sari te

　　　　shira ho kuru

Last year and this year

　　the boat with a black sail leaves the port

　　　　the boat with a white sail arrives at the port

Season word: *kozo kotoshi* (*lit.*, "last year and new year" means reminiscing about the last year on New Year's Day; new year)

Umi to yama (The Sea and the Mountain)

What comes from the sea?

Summer, wind, fish, and a basket of bananas
come from the sea.

Riding on the newly built boat,
the Sumiyoshi Festival also comes from the sea.

What comes from the mountain?

Winter, snow, little birds, and a horse
carrying charcoal come from the mountain.

Riding on the false daphne leaves,
New Year's Day also comes from the mountain.[6]

False daphne (yuzuriha, *daphniphyllum macropodum*) leaves are
used as New Year's Day ornaments.

淋しい少女

　　山の彼方の

　　　　お正月

Samishii shōjo

　　yama no kanata no

　　　　o shōgatsu

The lonely girl

　　looks for New Year's Day

　　　　in the mountains far away

Season word: *shōgatsu* (New Year's Day; new year)

Hiru to yoru (The Day and the Night)

Night comes after day.

Day comes after night.

Where can I see,

the long, long rope

and its ends?[7]

年新た

　　長き月日を

　　　　また生きる

Toshi arata

　　nagaki tsukihi o

　　　　mata ikiru

The new year has come

　　the woman thinks of the long days and months

　　　　of the year that she has to live

Season word: *toshi arata* (the new year has come; new year)

Hanabi II (The Fireworks II)

On the night of powder snow,
I passed through the shadow of the dead willow,
carrying an umbrella.

Then I suddenly remembered the fireworks
that I lit in the shadow of the willow
on the summer night.

I wish I had fireworks
that I can set off in the falling snow.
I want such fireworks.

On the night of powder snow,
as I pass through the shadow of the dead willow,
carrying an umbrella,

I can smell the fireworks
that I lit a long time ago.[8]

かまくらや

　　笑顔を灯す

　　　　紅き蝋燭

Kamakura ya

　　egao o tomosu

　　　　akaki rōsoku

The snow house

　　the smile of the child

　　　　glows in the red candlelight

Season word: *kamakura* (a small snow house for a Shinto ritual; new year)
Kamakura is a Shinto ritual for the "Small New Year's Day" (January 15 in the old calendar) mainly conducted in the northern snow country, such as Akita prefecture and also refers to the snow house itself that looks like an igloo of the Inuit.

Kan no ame (The Rain in the Coldest Season)

In the drizzling rain,
in the rain at dusk,
the yet unlit streetlight
is wet.

Yesterday's kite
is left as it was,
high up at the tip of the tree,
broken and wet.

Carrying the heavy umbrella
on my shoulder,
I am returning home,
carrying the medicine.

In the drizzling rain,
in the rain at dusk,
the mandarin orange peels
are stepped on and are wet.[9]

寒の入り

　　せせらぎの音の

　　　　氷りたり

Kan no iri

　　seseragi no ne no

　　　　kōri tari

The beginning of the coldest season

　　the sound of the waves on the river

　　　　is frozen

Season word: *kan no iri* (the beginning of the coldest season; winter)
"Kan no iri" (the beginning of the coldest season) usually falls on January 6, and this season lasts until February 3.

Yama to sora (The Mountain and the Sky)

If the mountain were made of glass,

I could see Tokyo.

    —As my big brother did

        who went to Tokyo on the train.

If the sky were made of glass,

I could see the gods.

    —As my little sister did

        who became an angel in heaven.[10]

It appears that "big brother" alludes to Misuzu's younger brother Masasuke, who moved to Tokyo and that "little sister" alludes to her bosom friend, Koeda (née Tanabe) Hohoyo (1903–July 1925), who died young after giving birth to her child.

仙崎の

　　冬空に映ゆ

　　　　友の顔

Senzaki no

　　fuyu zora ni hayu

　　　　tomo no kao

In Senzaki

　　the winter sky reflects

　　　　the face of her dead friend

Season word: *fuyu zora* (winter sky; winter)

Senzaki is Misuzu's birthplace, in Nagato, Yamaguchi prefecture.

Gakkō II: Hito ni okuru (The School II: Dedicated to a Person)

When the ice melts
you can see the school
at the bottom of the lake.

Ah, the red rooftiles and the white walls
were gently swaying,
reflected under the shadow of the reed blades.

The reeds died
and the school was demolished.

But when the ice melts
you can see the old shadow of the school
on the lake.

When the reeds grow again
you can hear the school bell ringing
at the bottom of the lake someday.[11]

This could have been dedicated to Misuzu's best friend, Koeda (née Tanabe) Hohoyo (1903–July 1925).

湖凍る

　　湖底に眠る

　　　　故郷よ

Umi kōru

　　kotei ni nemuru

　　　　fususato yo

The lake freezes

　　the hometown

　　　　lies at the bottom of the lake

Season word: *umi kōru* (lake freezes; winter)
During the age of hydropower dam construction in the 1960s, residents at the construction sites were forcibly evacuated and many communities ended up at the bottoms of dam lakes, including the villages by the Shō River in Gifu prefecture.

February

Photograph 2. Senzaki seen from Mt. Ōji, Ōmi Island, Nagato, Yamaguchi prefecture, August 2012, © Meg Itoh.

Yoru no yuki (The Snow at Night)

In the town where the heavy wet snow
and the light snow are falling,
there are a blind man and a child.

The piano is singing in the lit window.

The blind man stops his cane and listens to it.
The heavy wet snow falls on his hands.

The child looks at the lit window.
The heavy wet snow decorates her short-cut hair.

With all its heart for the two,
the piano sings the song of the springtime.

The heavy wet snow and the light snow
are falling on the two, gently and beautifully.[12]

牡丹雪

　　春の女神の

　　　　瞬きす

Botan yuki

　　haru no megami no

　　　　mabataki su

The heavy wet snow

　　the goddess of the spring

　　　　blinks

Season word: *botan yuki* (*lit.*, "peony snow," heavy wet snow; spring)

Awa yuki (The Light Snow)

It is snowing.

It is snowing.

As it falls, it disappears.

It is falling to become a mudpuddle.

The elder brother snow is falling.

The elder sister snow is falling.

The younger brother snow is falling.

The younger sister snow is falling.

They are falling one after another.

They are falling,

as if they were having fun dancing.

They are falling to become a mudpuddle.[13]

淡雪や

    稚児の睫毛に

        降りて消ゆ

Awa yuki ya

    chigo no matsuge ni

        furi te kiyu

The light snow

    descended on the girl's eyelashes

        and disappeared

Season word: *awa yuki* (light snow; spring)

Nukarumi (The Mudpuddle)

In the mudpuddle

in the back alley

there was a blue sky.

There was a beautiful

and clear sky

very far away.

The mudpuddle

in the back alley

was a deep sky.[14]

春潜む

　　どん底のより

　　　　深き処に

Haru hisomu

　　donzoko no yori

　　　　fukaki tokoro ni

Spring is hiding

　　deeper than

　　　　the lower depths

Season word: *haru* (spring; spring)

Aka-tsuchi yama (The Red Soil Mountain)

The red soil
on the red soil mountain
was sold
and carried to the town.

The red pine trees
on the red soil mountain
crumbled at their feet
and tilted.

Tilting and crying,
they saw off the horse cart,
carrying the red soil.

Under the glittering blue sky
and quietly on the white road,

the horse cart went far away,
carrying the red soil
that was sold to the town.[15]

松芽吹く

　　赤土売られ

　　　　芽の萎む

Matsu mebuku

　　aka tsuchi urare

　　　　me no shibomu

The pine tree budded

　　the red soil was sold

　　　　and the tree buds shriveled

Season word: *mebuku* (bud spouts; spring)

In Misuzu's poem, the "red pine trees" refer to *aka matsu* (Japanese red pine trees).

Tsuchi (The Soil)

Thunk, thunk.
The soil that is turned over
will become a good field
that will produce good wheat.

The soil that is stepped on
from morning to evening
will become a good road
that will let cars run.

The soil that is not turned over
the soil that is not stepped on
are they unnecessary?

No, no,
they will become
a home for nameless plants.[16]

麦踏みや

　　農夫の誓ひ

　　　　堅固なり

Mugi fumi ya

　　nōfu no chikai

　　　　kengo nari

Stepping on the wheatfield

　　the farmer's pledge for a good crop

　　　　becomes even firmer

Season word: *mugi fumi* (stepping on a wheatfield in order to strengthen and spread the roots; spring)

Hatake no ame (The Rain on the Field)

The spring rain

on the large-white radish field.

It falls on the green leaves

and smiles with a soft voice.

The daytime rain

on the large-white radish field.

It falls on the red sand soil

and sinks into the soil

quietly and lonelily.[17]

芽起こしの雨

　若菜も古菜も

　　嬉しかり

Meokoshi no ame

　wakana mo furuna mo

　　ureshi kari

The bud-inducing spring rain

　the vegetables—young and old—

　　must be happy

Season word: *meokoshi no ame* (the early spring rain that induces budding; spring)

Ashita (Tomorrow)

I saw the mother and daughter in town

and happened to hear them say

"Tomorrow."

The sunset glows at the end of the town.

Spring is coming around the corner

today.

I somehow felt happy

and also thought of

"Tomorrow."[18]

翌檜や

　春の光に

　　檜見る

Asunaro ya

　haru no hikari ni

　　hinoki miru

The young false arborvitae tree

　looks up at the hinoki cypress tree

　　in the spring light

Season word: *haru no hikari* (spring light; spring)
This alludes to a popular song about a young "asunaro" (*lit.*, "to become it tomorrow"), or a false arborvitae tree (a species of the cypress family), wishing to become a real hinoki cypress when it grows up.

Ōji-yama (Mt. Ōji)

All the cherry trees died
that had been planted to create the park,

but from all the stumps of the old trees
that had been cut down to create the park,
new buds sprouted and grew.

The silver sea is shining through the trees.
My hometown floats in the sea
like the Palace of the Dragon God of the Sea.

The silver rooftiles and stonewalls
look hazy like a dream.

If I looked down from Mt. Ōji,
I could like my hometown.

No smell of the dried sardines reaches here,
only the smell of the young tree buds fills the air.[19]

由藥や

　　海に浮かびし

　　　　竜宮城

Yūgetsu ya

　　umi ni ukabishi

　　　　Ryūgū jō

The new tree buds on Mt. Ōji

　　the Dragon Palace

　　　　is floating on the sea

Season word: *yūgetsu* (*hikobae*, basal shoots, new tree buds growing on old tree trunks or at the roots; spring) Mt. Ōji on Ōmi Island overlooks Misuzu's birthplace, Senzaki, Yamaguchi prefecture, which was a fishing village, and is one of the Eight Scenic Sites of Senzaki. Seen from Mt. Ōji, Senzaki looks like an island floating on the sea.

Tsuchi to kusa (The Soil and the Grass)

The [mother] soil raises alone

several tens of millions of grass seedlings,

who do not know

who their mother is.

The soil raises them

even if they will hide it,

when they grow up

and become lush green.[20]

母子草

　　その花言葉は

　　　　無償の愛

Hahako gusa

　　sono hana kotoba wa

　　　　mushō no ai

The Jersey cudweed

　　its flower language

　　　　is self-sacrificing love

Season word: *hahako-gusa* (*lit.*, "mother and child plant," Jersey cudweed; spring)

Hanazura (Hanazura Bay)

As I watched Hanazura Bay from the beach,
I heard the voice say "Once upon a time…"

Each time I see Hanazura Bay,
I think of him, feeling lonely.

I wonder where he is now
and what he is doing.

The postmaster who said "Once upon a time…"
and told me the story of Hanazura Bay.

Passing the tip of the bay,
the boat disappeared, far away.

The sea is burning in the sunset now, as it used to.
The boat is sailing on the sea now, as it used to.

Ah, "Once upon a time…"
Ah, Hanazura.

All became "Once upon a time…"[21]

花津浦

 椿吹かれて

  鳥の啼く

Hanazu ura

 tsubaki fukare te

  tori no naku

Hanazura Bay

 the camellia was blown by the wind

  and the bird cries

Season word: *tsubaki* (Japanese camellia; spring)

Hanazu Bay is one of the Eight Scenic Sites of Senzaki, Nagato, Yamaguchi prefecture.

Benten-jima (Benten Island)

"It is such a cute island,
it is too nice to be here,
so I shall tie it to my boat
and take it with me."

Said a fisherman
from the north country
one day, laughing.

I kept telling myself that it was a lie,
but I kept worrying in the dark night.

I rushed to the beach in the morning,
with my heart pounding.

There I found Benten Island
floating on the waves,
wrapped in golden light
and as green as before.[22]

春光や

　　弁天島の

　　　　夢物語

Shunkō ya

　　Benten jima no

　　　　yume monogatari

The spring light

　　the girl is imagining a story

　　　　about Benten Island

Season word: *shunkō* (spring light; spring)

Benten Island on Senzaki Bay is one of the Eight Scenic Sites of Senzaki, Nagato, Yamaguchi prefecture.

Sō-shun (Early Spring)

The handball came flying

accompanied

by the child.

The kite is floating

accompanied

by the boat whistling from the sea.

The spring came flying

accompanied

by the blue sky of today.

My heart is floating

accompanied

by the strikingly white moon far away.[23]

燕来る

　　いつもの村の

　　　　いつもの家に

Tsubame kuru

　　itsumo no mura no

　　　　itsumo no ie ni

The swallow has arrived

　　at the same old house

　　　　in the same old village

Season word: *tsubame kuru* (swallow arrives; spring)

Swallows migrate from the south to Japan every spring.

March

Photograph 3. Full moon in the spring.

Hi no hikari (The Sunlight)

Messengers of the sun left the sky together.
The southern wind met them on the street and asked,
"Where are you going? What for?"

One messenger answered,
"I am going to scatter this 'light' on the earth,
so that everyone can work."

Another messenger looked very happy and said,
"I am going to make flowers bloom,
so that the world can be a fun place."

Another messenger looked gentle and calm and said,
"I am going to build an arch bridge,
so that pure souls can climb up to heaven."

The last messenger looked lonely and said,
"I am still going with them,
in order to make a 'shadow.'"[24]

春の風

　　淋しき影を

　　　　そっと撫で

Haru no kaze

　　sabishiki kage o

　　　　sotto nade

The spring wind

　　gently blows on

　　　　the lonely shadow

Season word: *haru no kaze* (spring wind; spring)

Uchi umi soto umi (Inner Sea and Outer Sea)

The inner sea is rustling.
The outer sea is roaring.

The inner sea is a field of sand.
The outer sea is a field of rock.

The inner sea is light green.
The outer sea is dark blue.

The inner sea is mean.
The outer sea is angry.

The inner sea is a girl.
The outer sea is a boy.

They quarrel at the strait
and make a whirlpool.[25]

渦潮や

　　恋する女の

　　　　胸疼く

Uzu shio ya

　　koi suru hito no

　　　　mune uzuku

The whirlpool

　　the heart of the woman in love

　　　　is swirling

Season word: *uzu shio* (whirlpool; spring)

Seto no ame (The Whirlpool at the Strait)

Drizzle falls and stops.

The ferry goes and comes back.

The two tides meet at the strait.

"Are you going that way?"

"I am going this way. Good-bye."

They circle around and make a whirlpool.

The ferry goes and comes back.

Drizzle falls and stops.[26]

渦潮よ

  乙女の涙

    飲み込まん

Uzu shio yo

  otome no namida

    nomikoman

The whirlpool

  swallows up

    the tears of the maiden

Season word: *uzu shio* (whirlpool; spring)

Komatsubara (Komatsubara)

In Komatsubara,
the pine trees have become scarce.

The same old wood sawyer
is sawing a large piece of wood.

Each time he pushes and pulls
the white sail appears and disappears.

The gull is flying over the waves.
The lark is singing in the sky.

It is spring in the sea and the sky,
but the pine trees and the wood sawyer seem sad.

New houses are being built
here and there.

In Komatsubara,
the pine trees have become scarce.[27]

小松原

　　木挽の吐息

　　　　雲雀聴く

Komatsubara

　　kobiki no toiki

　　　　hibari kiku

Komatsubara

　　the lone wood sawyer sighs

　　　　and the lark listens

Season word: *hibari* (lark; spring)

Komatsubara, a pine grove on the pebble beach located on the east coast of Senzaki, is one of the Eight Scenic Sites of Senzaki.

Nami no hashidate (Nami no hashidate)

Nami no hashidate is a fine place.
To the right is the lake where the grebe [bird] dives.
To the left is the outer sea where the white sail passes.

The pine grove in between is Komatsubara,
where the breeze passes through gently.

>The gull on the sea
>plays with the duck on the lake
>and passes the day.

>When the blue moon rises
>the lord of the lake
>collects shellfish at the beach.

Nami no hashidate is a fine place.
To the right is the lake where the waves are calm.
To the left is the outer sea where the waves are violent.

The pebble beach in between is Koishibara,
where the wooden clogs pass through clattering.[28]

麗らかに

　　海辺に游ぶ

　　　　鳥と貝

Uraraka ni

　　umibe ni asobu

　　　　tori to kai

The gentle, beautiful spring

　　the little bird and the shellfish

　　　　are playing at the beach

Season word: *uraraka* (gentle, beautiful spring; spring) Nami no hashidate (a sandbar), located on the southwest part of Ōmi Island is one of the Eight Scenic Sites of Senzaki. In this poem, Ko-i<u>shi</u>-bara (pebble field) is a pun on Ko-matsu-bara" (pine field). This is a different Komatsubara from the Komatsubara on the east coast of Senzaki. The grebe (waterfowl) is called "moguccho" (diver) in the local dialect.

O-nen'ne o-fune (The Sleeping Boat)

The boat that came
from the island seems tired.
It is sleeping comfortably
in the gentle waves at the cove.

That small boat came
from the violent and vast sea,
carrying fish from far away.
It is sleeping.

When fishermen
from the island sail back,
they buy a heavy bag of rice,
they buy green vegetables.

Till then, the boat that came
from the island
is sleeping comfortably
swung by the gentle waves.[29]

春の月

　　優しき波の

　　　　子守唄

Haru no tsuki

　　yasashiki nami no

　　　　komori uta

The spring moon

　　the gentle waves sing

　　　　the lullaby to the small boat

Season word: *haru no tsuki* (spring moon; spring)

In Misuzu's poem, the island refers to Ōmi Island, the birthplace of her father, across the strait from Senzaki.

Ho I (The Sails I)

The sails of the boats
that arrived at the port
are all old and black,

but the sails of the boats
that sail the sea far away
are all shining and white.

The boats far away in the sea
never arrive at the port,

but always sail on the border
between the sea and the sky
and sail far away.

They sail away shining.[30]

春の雲

　　真白き鴎

　　　　波と帆と

Haru no kumo

　　ma shiroki kamome

　　　　nami to ho to

The spring clouds

　　the pure white gulls

　　　　are playing with the waves and the sails

Season word: *haru no kumo* (spring clouds; spring)

Fune no o-uchi (The Boat Home)

My father,

my mother,

my elder brother,

and I aboard,

the boat home is fun.

We unloaded the shipments

and the sun has set.

When the Evening Star shines

on the sail mast of the boat next to ours,

we listen to my father's stories

by the red-burning wood

and fall asleep.

When the Morning Star rises,

we raise the sail

in the morning breeze

and leave the port off

to the big sea.

When the morning mist clears,

an island appears.

When the waves shine,

the fish fly.

The wind began to blow

in the afternoon

and the waves swell up and rise.

When the golden sun sets

at the far end of the sea,

the sea is prettier than flowers.

We eat the rice cooked with sea water.

The sun is shining all over the boat.

The wind is blowing all over the sail.

We travel across the big sea.

The boat home is fun.[31]

春の海

　　明けの明星

　　　　舟起こす

Haru no umi

　　ake no myōjō

　　　　fune okosu

The spring sea

　　the Morning Star

　　　　wakes up the boat

Season word: *haru no umi* (spring sea; spring)

Ii koto (The Good Things)

The place where

the old mud wall crumbled and

I can see the head of the grave.

The place where

I can see the sea first

at the edge of the mountain

on the right of the road.

I feel happy

whenever I pass by the place

where I did a good thing.[32]

The grave refers to that of Misuzu's maternal grandfather whom she never met.

風光る

    少女の心

        跳ね躍る

Kaze hikaru

    shojō no kokoro

        hane odoru

The shining wind

    the girl's heart

        is bouncing with joy

Season word: *kaze hikaru* (the wind shines; spring)

Haka tachi (My Dear Gravestones)

A fence is being created
at the back of the graveyard.

The gravestones can no longer see
the sea afterward.

They can no longer see boats come and go,
with the children of their children aboard.

A fence is being created
on the coastal road.

We can no longer see
the gravestones afterward.

We can no longer see the smallest,
round one, the favorite one that
I always look at when I pass by.[33]

春の空

　　祖父眠る墓

　　　　見遣りたり

Haru no sora

　　sofu nemuru haka

　　　　miyari tari

The spring sky

　　watches over the grave

　　　　of Misuzu's grandfather

Season word: *haru no sora* (spring sky; spring)

In Misuzu's poem, her favorite grave refers to that of her maternal grandfather whom she never met.

Umi e (To the Sea)

My grandfather went to the sea,

so did my father,

so did my elder brother,

so did everyone, everyone.

Beyond the sea

is a good place,

for once everyone has gone,

they never came back.

I too fast become a grownup,

and go to the sea also.[34]

春彼岸

   みすゞの願ひ

      いよ強し

Haru higan

   Misuzu no negai

      iyo tsuyoshi

The spring equinox

   Misuzu's wish

      becomes stronger

Season word: *haru higan* (spring equinox; spring)

Misuzu might have wished to go to heaven to join her father and grandfather there on this Buddhist memorial day.

April

Photograph 4. Coneflower with bees.

Ohi-san, ame-san (The Sun and the Rain)

The rain washed down

the dust from the turf grass.

The sun dried up

the rain from the turf grass.

So that I could lie down on it

and watch the sky like this.[35]

春の野や

　　光と少女

　　　　追ひかける

Haru no no ya

　　hikari to shōjo

　　　　oikakeru

The spring field

　　the light and the girl

　　　　are playing tag

Season word: *haru no no* (spring field; spring)

Tsuyu (The Dewdrop)

I shall not tell anyone,

that a flower cried quietly

in the corner of the garden

in the morning.

For if the rumor spreads

and the bee hears about it,

the bee will go back to the flower

and return the nectar,

as if it had done something wrong.[36]

蜂と花

みすゞの心

愛しむ

Hachi to hana

Misuzu no kokoro

itsuku shimu

The bee and the flower

embrace

the heart of Misuzu

Season word: *hachi* (bee; spring)

Sora to umi (The Sky and the Sea)

The spring sky shines.

It shines like silk.

Why, why does it shine?

For it has stars inside.

The spring sea shines.

It shines like a seashell.

Why, why does it shine?

For it has pearls inside.[37]

春日和

　　仙崎の海

　　　　しばし微睡む

Haru biyori

　　Senzaki no umi

　　　　shibashi madoromu

The fine spring day

　　the sea in Senzaki

　　　　is dozing off for a while

Season word: *haru biyori* (fine spring day; spring)

Haru no o-hata (The Weaver of the Spring)

"Ton, ton, tonkararin." [tapping sound]
Princess Saho weaved long time ago.

Turning the wheat into green,
the rapeseed into yellow,
the milkvetch into red,
and the mist into white.

Out of the five colors of thread,
she used four,
and only the blue thread remained.

"Ton, ton, tonkararin."
Using the blue thread,
Princess Saho wove the sky.[38]

Princess Saho was a goddess and a deification of Mt. Saho in Nara, which symbolized spring.

93

チューリップ

　　五色の風を

　　　　織り交ぜる

Chūrippu

　　goshiki no kaze o

　　　　ori mazeru

The tulips

　　are weaving

　　　　five different colors of wind

Season word: *chūrippu* (tulip; spring)

Shigastu (April)

The new book

in the new schoolbag.

The new leaf

on the new branch.

The new sun

in the new sky.

The new April

and happy April.[39]

The Japanese schoolyear begins in April.

新入生

　　ランドセルの匂ひ

　　　　背負ひたり

Shin'nyūsei

　　randoseru no nioi

　　　　seoi tari

The first grader

　　carries the scent

　　　　of the new leather backpack

Season word: *shin'nyūsei* (first grader in April; spring)

Ikken-ya no tokei (The Clock in the Isolated House)

The sun sits

in the middle of the sky.

The lazy clock

is lagging behind.

Let's adjust it

to the sun.

The clock

in the isolated house

in the country

is yawning and napping

all day long.[40]

風優し

　　日永一日

　　　　夢見る娘

Kaze yasashi

　　hinaga ichinichi

　　　　yume miru ko

The gentle breeze

　　the girl is daydreaming

　　　　on a long spring day

Season word: *hinaga* (a long spring day; spring)

Watashi no oka ([Good-bye] My Hill)

Good-bye my hill.

The green grass on my hill,
where I used to pick
the ears of cogon grass,

and blow on the grass-reed,
looking at the blue sky,
I wish you all grow well.

Even if I am gone,
all the others will come to the hill
and play again.

The weakling who was lost and alone
may call it "my hill,"
just as I used to.

But for me,
it is "my hill" forever.

Good-bye my hill.[41]

茅花抜く

　　童の口と

　　　　手の青よ

Tsubana nuku

　　warabe no kuchi to

　　　　te no ao yo

Picking the ears of cogon grass

　　the mouth and the hands of the child

　　　　are all green

Season word: *tsubana nuku* (to pick the ears of cogon grass, *imperata cylindrica*; spring)
Tsubana (*lit.*, "flower of chigaya," ears of cogon grass) is related to sugarcane, and Japanese children used to chew the tender ears.

O-tento-san no uta (The Song of the Sun)

The Japanese national flag

is the flag of the sun.

The Japanese children

are the children of the sun.

Let the children sing

the song of the sun

under the cherry blossoms

and at the bottom of the spring haze.

Let's load the song

that overflows Japan onto the boat

and distribute it all over the world.

Let's sing the song of the sun

in the shadows of the cherry blossoms

and under the sun so that it shall overflow.[42]

花の宴

　　稚児の歌声

　　　　空の笑む

Hana no en

　　chigo no utagoe

　　　　sora no emu

The cherry blossom viewing party

　　the children's singing

　　　　makes the sky smile

Season word: *hana no en* (cherry blossom viewing party; spring)
In haiku, "hana" (flower) refers to cherry blossoms, as they are representative flowers of Japan.

Akai o-fune (The Red Boat)

A lone pine tree,

it stands alone and watches the sea.

I also watch the sea alone.

The sea is sheer blue,

the cloud is white.

I cannot see the red boat yet.

My father in the red boat,

my father in my dream in the past,

lone pine tree, lone pine tree,

when will he come?[43]

一本松

　　春の潮に

　　　　立つ子待つ

Ippon matsu

　　haru no ushio ni

　　　　tatsu ko matsu

The lone pine tree

　　waits for the child

　　　　standing alone by the spring tide

Season word: *haru no ushio* (spring tide; spring)

Gakkō I (The School I)

Some came by ferry,
some came crossing mountains.

Behind, there was a mountain, with cicada chirps.
In front, there was a riverbank, with wind in the reeds.

Beyond the rice paddies, there was the sea,
with upright-sail and tilted-sail boats.

When the snow disappeared from red rooftiles,
the peach trees blossomed in the blue sky.

When freshmen came,
grebes and frogs all sang.

Carrying a black wrap on my back,
I picked red strawberries.

Ah, my school with red rooftiles,
ah, the rooftiles that were reflected in the water.

They are only in my heart now,
like the shadows on the water.[44]

大津高女

　蛙の合唱

　　聞く校舎

Ōtsu kōjo

　kawazu no gasshō

　　kiku kōsha

Ōtsu Higher Women's School

　the old school building

　　listens to the chorus of frogs

Season word: *kawazu* (*kaeru*, frog; spring)

In Misuzu's poem, grebes (nio, kaitsuburi) are waterfowl. Ōtsu Higher Women's School, in Nagato, Yamaguchi prefecture, was Misuzu's alma mater.

May

Photograph 5. Crescent moon.

Nami (The Waves)

The waves are children.

They come together

hand in hand and smiling.

The waves are erasers.

They erase all the letters

on the sand as they leave.

The waves are soldiers.

They attack from offshore

and shoot all at once.

The waves are forgetful.

They leave behind

pretty seashells on the beach.[45]

桜貝

　　白砂の浜の

　　　　花のごと

Sakura gai

　　hakusa no hama no

　　　　hana no goto

The pink seashell

　　lies on the white sand beach

　　　　as if it were the cherry blossom

Season word: *sakura gai* (pink seashell, *Nitidotellina nitidula*, a species of tellin; spring)

Ukishima (The Floating Island)

I wish I had an island.

It is a small floating island

that is swung by the waves.

The island is always full of flowers.

The small house has a roof with flowers.

It is floating,

making a shadow on the green sea.

If I grew tired of watching the sea,

I can jump into the sea,

dive under the island,

and play hide and seek.

I wish I had such a small island.[46]

春の波

　　赤き花藻の

　　　　揺らぎたり

Haru no nami

　　akaki hana mo no

　　　　yuragi tari

The spring waves

　　the red sea plant blossoms

　　　　are swaying gently

Season word: *haru no nami* (spring waves; spring)

Kaze (The Wind)

The goatherd in the sky

is invisible.

Having been driven there,

the goats are roaming

on the edge of the vast field

in the evening.

The goatherd in the sky

is invisible.

When the goats were dyed red

by the sunset,

he is blowing a whistle

far away.[47]

山笑ふ

  山羊と山羊追ひ

    雲を追ふ

Yama warau

  yagi to yagi oi

    kumo o ou

The mountain smiles

  the goats and the goatherd

    are herding the clouds

Season word: *yama warau* (mountain smiles; spring)

Doyō nichiyō (Saturday and Sunday)

Saturday is the leaf.

Sunday is the flower.

Tearing off the leaf

of the calendar on the house pillar,

Saturday evening

is a fun time.

But the flower

is soon to shrink.

Tearing off the flower

of the calendar on the house pillar,

Sunday evening

is a sad time.[48]

春風や

　　散り花拾ふ

　　　　娘と語る

Haru kaze ya

　　chiri bana hirou

　　　　ko to kataru

The spring wind

　　stops to talk with the girl

　　　　who is picking up the fallen flower petals

Season word: *haru kaze* (spring wind; spring)

Mō iino ("Are You Ready?")

—"Are you ready?"
— "Not yet."

Under the loquat tree
and in the shadow of the peony,
the children are playing hide and seek.

—"Are you ready?"
—"Not yet."

In the loquat tree branches
and among the green fruits,
the little bird and the loquat
are playing hide and seek.

—"Are you ready?"
—"Not yet."

Outside the sky
and inside the black soil
the summer and the spring
are playing hide and seek.[49]

雛巣立つ
　　光と風と
　　　　隠れんぼ

Hina sudatsu
　　hikari to kaze to
　　　　kakurenbo

The chicks have fledged
　　they are playing hide and seek
　　　　with the light and the wind

Season word: *hina sudatsu* (chicks fledged; spring)

Inaka (The Countryside)

I am dying to see.

The little mandarin oranges
ripened golden on the tree.

The baby figs
hanging on to the tree.

And the wind blowing on the wheat spikes
and the lark singing.

I am dying to go.

I know that the lark sings in the spring,
but I wonder when the mandarin orange tree blossoms
and what the blossoms look like.

In the countryside
that I only see in the picture,
there must be many, many things
that are not in the picture.[50]

花蜜柑

　　みすゞに届け

　　　その香り

Hana mikan

　　Misuzu ni todoke

　　　sono kaori

Mandarin orange blossoms

　　Send your fragrance

　　　to Misuzu!

Season word: *hana mikan* (mandarin orange blossoms; summer)

In haiku, May 5 marks the beginning of summer.

Yonaka no kaze (The Wind at Midnight)

The wind at midnight is naughty.

Because if it passes through alone, it is lonely.

It wonders if it should blow the leaves of the pink silk tree.

But then they will be swung and fall asleep,

dreaming of sailing on the boat.

It wonders if it should blow the blades of grass.

But then they will be swung and fall asleep,

dreaming of playing on the swing.

The wind at midnight looks disappointed

and is passing through the sky alone.[51]

合歓の花

　　ねむのき学園

　　　　慈しむ

Nemu no hana

　　Nemu no ki gakuen

　　　　itsuku shimu

The pink silk tree blossoms

　　care for the children

　　　　at the Nemu-no-ki Academy

Season word: *nemu no hana* (*nemu no ki no hana*, pink silk tree blossoms; summer)

Pink silk tree (*lit.*, "nemu no ki," sleeping tree) leaves close at night; hence the name. Their flowers are fragrant. Nemu-no-ki Academy is a school for disabled children founded in 1968 in Kakegawa, Shizuoka prefecture, by the actress Miyagi Mariko (1927–2020).

Utsukushii machi (The Beautiful Town)

Suddenly, I remembered

the red roofs by the riverbank

in that town.

And the white sail

on the big blue river,

moving very quietly.

And the young male painter

on the grass of the riverbank,

looking at the water absentmindedly.

And then, what was I doing?

I could not remember at first, but

it was an illustration in a book

that I had borrowed from someone.[52]

夏の空

　　夢想に耽る

　　　　娘と絵描き

Natsu no sora

　　musō ni fukeru

　　　　ko to ekaki

The summer sky

　　the girl and the painter

　　　　are immersed in their daydreams

Season word: *natsu no sora* (summer sky; summer)

Aki yashiki no ishi (The Stones at the Empty House)

The stones at the empty house

are gone.

They were handy

for pounding the birdlime, indeed.

The stones were carried

by the horse cart.

The grass at the empty house

looks lonely, indeed.[53]

Birdlime is an adhesive, made of sticky tree bark and fruits, to catch birds and insects.

廃屋に

　　生ひ茂る

　　　　クイーン・アンズ・レース

Haioku ni

　　oi shigeru

　　　　kuiin anzu rēsu

In the abandoned house

　　the Queen Anne's lace

　　　　is taking over quietly

Season word: *kuiin anzu rēsu* (Queen Anne's lace, wild carrot; summer)

Kuregata II (Dusk II)

The red window on the dark mountain,

what is inside the window?

There is an empty baby crib

and a mother in tears.

The golden moon in the light sky,

what is on the moon?

There is a golden crib

and a baby in slumber.[54]

夏の宵

　　揺り籠優し

　　　　三日月よ

Natsu no yoi

　　yurikago yasashi

　　　　mikazuki yo

The summer evening

　　the crescent moon

　　　　is gently swaying the baby crib

Season word: *natsu no yoi* (summer evening; summer)

June

Photograph 6. Rainbow.

Umi no hate (The End of the Sea)

The cloud emerges from there.

The rainbow also rises from there.

I want to go there on a boat someday.

I want to go to the end of the sea.

Even if it were too far,

and it became sundown,

and I could not see anything.

I want to go to the end of the sea,

where I can pick stars in my hand,

like I pick red jujubes.[55]

海の果て

　　夢の小舟の

　　　　虹と消ゆ

Umi no hate

　　yume no ko bune no

　　　　niji to kiyu

At the end of the sea

　　the small dream boat

　　　　has disappeared into the rainbow

Season word: *niji* (rainbow; summer)

Hikari no kago (The Cage of Light)

I am a little bird now.

In the cage of light

in the summer tree shade,

it is owned by someone

and sings all the songs it knows.

I am such a cute little bird.

The cage of light breaks

if it just spreads its wings.

But it is obedient

and stays in the cage and sings.

I am such a gentle-hearted little bird.[56]

夏木立

　　金の小鳥の

　　　　歌光る

Natsu kodachi

　　kin no kotori no

　　　　uta hikaru

In the shade of summer trees

　　the song of the golden bird

　　　　is shining

Season word: *natsu kodachi* (summer tree shade; summer)

Manbai (Ten Thousand Times)

It is ten thousand times prettier than

all the palaces of the kings in the world combined

—the night sky adorned with stars.

It is ten thousand times prettier than

all the dresses of the queens of the world combined

—the morning rainbow reflected in the water.

It is ten thousand times prettier than

even the night sky adorned with stars

and the morning rainbow reflected in the water combined

—the land of the gods beyond the sky.[57]

朝の虹

　　少女の夢を

　　　　架ける橋

Asa no niji

　　shōjo no yume o

　　　　kakeru hashi

The morning rainbow

　　is making the bridge

　　　　to bring the girl's dreams to her

Season word: *niji no asa* (morning rainbow; summer)

O-tsuitachi (The First Day [of June])

The first day, the first day [of June].

It is a very pretty morning sky.

I am wearing a single-layered kimono from today.

The first day, the first day.

The policeman is also wearing a white uniform

on which a black funeral armband stands out.

The first day, the first day.

A monk will come for a prayer service later this evening

and the sweet offerings will be passed down to us later.

The first day, the first day.

It is a splendid day.

Summer begins in the town today.[58]

更衣

　　十二単衣の

　　　　姫の汗

Koromo gae

    jūni hitoe no

        hime no ase

The season for changing to summer clothes

    the sweat of the princess

        who wore a twelve-layered kimono

Season words: *koromo gae* (the season for changing to summer clothes; summer) and *ase* (sweat; summer)
In Misuzu's poem, "tsuitachi" refers to the first day of the month, but also to 'June' specifically in the old calendar.

Niji to hikōki (The Rainbow and the Airplane)

The townsfolk saw the rainbow

for the first time.

They saw it

when they went out to see the airplane.

In the drizzling sky,

the airplane

is flying into the ring of the rainbow

in a hurry.

Oh, I see,

Oh, I see,

the airplane was sent from the rainbow

so that the townsfolk could see it.[59]

二重虹

　　ワイキキを飛ぶ

　　　　ジェット二機

Futae niji

　　Waikiki o tobu

　　　　jetto niki

The double rainbow

　　two jet airplanes are flying

　　　　over Waikiki beach

Season word: *futae niji* (double rainbow; summer)

Hawaii is known for frequent appearance of rainbows and is referred to as the "Rainbow State."

Matsuge no niji (The Rainbows on My Eyelashes)

Wiping my tears that keep welling up,

no matter how many times I wipe them,

I wonder

—if I must have been an adopted child—

Watching the beautiful rainbows

on the edges of my eyelashes,

I wonder

—what is the afternoon snack today?—[60]

紫陽花や

　　泣く子をなだめ

　　　　虹を呼ぶ

Ajisai ya

　　naku ko o nadame

　　　　niji o yobu

The hydrangea

　　consoles the crying girl

　　　　and sends for the rainbow

Season words: *ajisai* (hydrangea; summer) and *niji* (rainbow; summer)

Mizu to kage (The Water and the Shadow)

The shadow of the sky
is everywhere on the water.

At the edge of the sky,
the trees are reflected
and the wild roses are also reflected.

The water is obedient.
It reflects every shadow.

The shadow of the water
is reflected in the thicket of trees
here and there.

It is light,
it is cool, and
it is swaying.

The water is decent.
Its own shadow is small.[61]

野茨や

　　水面に散りて

　　　　影となる

Noibara ya

　　minamo ni chiri te

　　　　kage to naru

The wild rose

　　its petals fall on the water

　　　　and become shadows

Season word: *noibara* (wild rose; summer)

Kai to tsuki (The Seashell and the Moon)

Immersed in the dyeing pot,

the white thread becomes dark blue.

Immersed in the blue ocean,

why does the white seashell remain white?

Immersed in the sunset sky,

the white cloud becomes red.

Immersed in the dark blue night sky,

why does the white moon remain white?[62]

夏の月

　　眠る真珠に

　　　　囁けり

Natsu no tsuki

　　nemuru shinju ni

　　　　sasayakeri

The summer moon

　　whispered to the pearls

　　　　sleeping in the sea

Season word: *natsu no tsuki* (summer moon; summer)

Fushigi (I Wonder)

I cannot stop wondering

why the rain that falls from the black clouds

shines silver.

I cannot stop wondering

why the silkworm that eats green mulberry leaves

becomes white.

I cannot stop wondering

why the white-flowered gourd that nobody touches

opens its petals by itself.

I cannot stop wondering

why everyone I asked laughed

and said, "It's natural."[63]

桑の実や

    小鳥と子供

        紅き口

Kuwa no mi ya

    kotori to kodomo

        akaki kuchi

The mulberries

    the bird and the child

        their mouths turned red

Season word: *kuwa no mi* (mulberries; summer)

Hama no ishi (The Pebbles at the Beach)

The pebbles at the beach are like beads.

All are round and slippery.

The pebbles at the beach are like flying fish.

When thrown they go across the waves swiftly.

The pebbles at the beach are singers.

They sing with the waves all day long.

Each one of the pebbles at the beach

is little and cute.

But the pebbles at the beach are great stones.

Together they hold the vast sea.[64]

夏の浜

　　リフレインする

　　　　さざなみの唄

Natsu no hama

　　rifurein suru

　　　　sazanami no uta

The summer beach

　　the song of the gentle waves

　　　　sings gentle refrains

Season word: *natsu no hama* (summer beach; summer)

Kiri ishi (The Cut Stone)

The stone

that was cut by the stonecutter

flew into the puddle

on the street.

The barefoot child,

who is going home from school

walking on the left of the street,

"Watch out."

Having been cut,

the stone is angry.[65]

夕立や

　　石の怒りを

　　　　鎮め往く

Yūdachi ya

　　ishi no ikari o

　　　　shizume yuku

The summer shower

　　cooled the anger

　　　　of the cut stone

Season word: *yūdachi* (summer shower; summer)

Kodomo to moguri to tsuki to (The Child, the Diver, and the Moon)

The child picks wildflowers in the field,
but scatters them on the road on her way home,
one petal at time.

When she returns home, she has none.

The diver collects corals in the sea,
but when she surfaces, she leaves them in the boat
and dives into the sea again, empty-handed.

She has none for herself.

The moon collects the stars in the sky,
but when it has passed the fifteenth night,
it scatters them in the sky, yet again.

It has none by the end of the month.[66]

アンタレス

 海女に捧げる

  赤珊瑚

Antaresu

 ama ni sasageru

  aka sango

Antares

 gives the female diver

  the red coral

Season word: *Antaresu* (Antares; summer)
Antares, of bright red color, is the alpha star of the constellation Scorpius. Ama (*lit.*, "sea woman") refers to female divers who collect marine products, such as pearl oysters. Red corals are prized as material for jewelry in Asia.

July

Photograph 7. Sea and sky, Ōmi Island, Nagato, Yamaguchi prefecture, August 2012, © Meg Itoh.

Shirayuri jima (The White Lily Island)

There is an isolated island far, far away
that only I know.
I always draw a map
in the shadow of the poplar tree at school.

The island will disappear when it is swept
and changes each time I draw it.
But it always has a lake in the middle
and always has a palace at the shore.

A princess lives in the palace
that is whiter than the snow and fragrant,
wearing a long pale-green gown
and wearing a golden tiara.

White lilies grow on the island, in full bloom.
Attracted by the fragrance of the lilies, white up to the sky,
a boat approaches the island,
but they all bloom on the cliff and cannot be picked.

I always draw a map
in the shadow of the green poplar leaves.
Never getting tired of it,
I draw a map of "White Lily Island" many times.[67]

白百合や

    乙女の霊を

        永遠に守らむ

Shira yuri ya

    otome no rei o

        towa ni mamoran

The white lily

    guards the souls of the maidens

        forever

Season word: *shira yuri* (white s lily; summer)
This is a memorial tribute to the Himeyuri no tō (Princess Lily Tower), dedicated to female students who were conscripted as nurses and were killed during the Battle of Okinawa in 1945.

Fushigi na minato (The Mysterious Seaport)

The big old clock at the seaport
was hung with 6 o'clock at the top.
The two hands were moving to the left
endlessly and strangely.

At the rotten, broken pier,
a bright red flower was swaying
in the daylight
alone.

On the black, quiet water,
the old ship was moored
quietly
like a mountain.

In which country
was there such a seaport?
When was it?

No one would know.
For it is in my dream.[68]

ハイビスカス

　　常夏の地に

　　　休む船

Haibisukasu

　　tokonatsu no chi ni

　　　yasumu fune

The hibiscus

　　watches the foreign ship

　　　anchored at a tropical land

Season word: *haibisukasu* (hibiscus; summer)

Sora no iro (The Color of the Sky)

The sea, the sea, why is it blue?

Because it reflects the sky.

When the sky is cloudy,

the sea also looks cloudy.

The sunset glory, the sunset glory, why is it red?

Because the setting sun is red.

But, why is it blue

although the sun in the daytime is not blue?

The sky, the sky, why is it blue?[69]

夏の空

　　海呑み込みて

　　　　海より青し

Natsu no sora

　　umi nomikomi te

　　　　umi yori aoshi

The summer sky

　　has swallowed up the sea

　　　　and became bluer than the sea

Season word: *natsu no sora* (summer sky; summer)

Kumo no iro (The Color of the Clouds)

The color of the clouds

after the sunset glory,

I came out alone,

after the quarrel,

As I was watching it,

I suddenly burst into tears.[70]

夕焼雲

　　鴉の子待つ

　　　　山となる

Yuyake gumo

　　karasu no ko matsu

　　　　yama to naru

The clouds in the sunset glory

　　disappeared into the mountains

　　　　where the crow chicks wait

Season word: *yuyake gumo* (clouds reflecting the sunset glory; summer)

Umi no iro (The Color of the Sea)

It is a glittering silver sea in the morning.

The silver makes everything black.

The color of the launches, the color of the sails,

and the color of the cracks in the silver, are all black.

It is a gentle blue sea in the daytime.

The blue is letting everything be as it is—

the floating straw scraps, the bamboo strips,

and the banana peels—are all as they are.

It is a quiet black sea at night.

The black covers everything.

I cannot tell if there is a boat or not.

The only thing I can see is the reflection of the red light.[71]

夏の海

　　銀の波間に

　　　　憩む鳥

Natsu no umi

　　gin no namima ni

　　　　yasumu tori

The summer sea

　　the birds are resting

　　　　on the silver waves

Season word: *natsu no umi* (summer sea; summer)

Hikaru kami (The Shining Hair)

It is sinking, it is sinking,

as I come to the beach.

It is the huge red sunset globe.

It is shining, it is shining,

the golden thread is shining.

It is the hair of Mitchan,

watching the sunset.

Let's hang it, let's hang it.

Let's hang the red globe

onto the hemp leaf

with the golden thread.[72]

夕焼に

　　光る童や

　　　　金の波

Yūyake ni

　　hikaru warabe ya

　　　　kin no nami

In the sunset glow

　　the child is shining

　　　　reflecting the golden waves

Season word: *yūyake* (sunset glow; summer)

Yoru (The Night)

The night puts black nightwear

on the mountains and the trees in the forests,

on the birds in the nests and the grass blades

and even on little red flowers.

But it cannot do so

only to me.

My nightwear is white.

My mother puts it on me.[73]

白き百合

　　夜の帳に

　　　　忍び咲く

Shiroki yuri

　　yoru no tobari ni

　　　　shinobi saku

The white lily

　　is blooming silently

　　　　in the dark at night

Season word: *shiroki yuri* (*shira yuri*, white lily; summer)

Nazo (The Puzzle)

What is the puzzle?

What is the thing that there is plenty of,

but you cannot catch?

      It is the blue water of the blue sea

      because if you scoop it, it is not blue.

What is the puzzle?

What is the thing that has no substance,

but you can catch?

      It is the breeze in the summer afternoon

      because you can catch it with a paper fan.[74]

炎帝や

　　空海の問ふ

　　　　空と海

Entei ya

　　Kūkai no tou

　　　　sora to umi

The burning sun

　　Kūkai is mediating

　　　　with the sky and the sea

Season word: *entei* (burning sun; summer)

Kūkai (774–835) is the founder of Shingon school Buddhism. His name literally means "the sky and the sea" after what he observed during his meditations.

Kumo I (The Cloud I)

I wish to become a cloud.

Then I could float in the blue sky,

see all of it from one end to the other,

and play tag with the moon at night.

If I grew tired of it,

I would become rain,

and jump into the pond of my house,

accompanied by thunder and lightning.[75]

仙崎よ

    雷お嬢の

        お帰りよ

Senzaki yo

    kaminari ojō no

        o kaeri yo

Senzaki !

    Little Miss Thunder and Lightning

        is coming home

Season word: *kaminari* (thunder and lightning; summer)

Senzaki is Misuzu's birthplace in Nagato, Yamaguchi prefecture.

Yūdachi seibatsu (Conquering the Summer Shower)

Loading the basin-boat

with the shining saber, the cedarwood gun,

and the biscuits

that my mother gave me for a snack,

Let's embark for sailing now.

The captain is boarding.

If the goldfish asks me on the way,

I shall shout in a dignified fashion.

"We are on our way to conquer

the summer shower

that smashed the miniature garden I had made,

and left."[76]

夕立や

　　金魚の池の

　　　　大津波

Yūdachi ya

　　kingyo no ike no

　　　　ō tsunami

The summer shower

　　has shaken the goldfish pond

　　　　like a big tsunami

Season words: *yūdachi* (summer shower; summer) and *kingyo* (goldfish; summer)

Aoi sora (The Blue Sky)

The empty sky,

the blue sky,

it looks like the sea

on a day without waves.

I wish

I could jump

right into the middle of it

and swim through it.

Then, this would make

a straight white bubble,

which would turn into

a cloud by itself.[77]

雲の峰

　福島の廃炉

　　より出る

Kumo no mine

　Fukushima no hairo

　　yori izuru

The towering cloud

　rises from

　　the abandoned nuclear power station

　　　in Fukushima

Season word: *kumo no mine* (towering cloud; cumulonimbus cloud; summer)

Kaya (The Mosquito Net)

Inside the mosquito net,

we are the fish caught in the net.

In the blue ocean under the blue moon,

a blue rope is floating on the waves.

While we were sound asleep,

an idle star came to pull up the mosquito net.

If we woke up in the middle of the night,

we would find ourselves sleeping

on the sand of the clouds.[78]

夏の夜を

　　游ぐ童の

　　　　夢枕

Natsu no yo o

　　oyogu warabe no

　　　　yume makura

The summer night

　　the children are dreaming

　　　　of swimming in the night sky

Season word: *natsu no yo* (summer night; summer)

August

Photograph 8. Goldfish.

Kodama de shōka (Are You an Echo?)

When I said, "Let's play,"

you said, "Let's play."

When I said, "You're silly,"

you said, "You're silly."

When I said, "I won't play with you anymore,"

you said, "I won't play with you anymore."

Then, I became lonely afterward.

When I said, "I'm sorry,"

you said, "I'm sorry."

Are you an echo?

No, it could be anyone.[79]

夏の山

 みすゞの叫び

  木霊聴く

Natsu no yama

 Misuzu no sakebi

  kodama kiku

The summer mountain

 Misuzu's cries for help

  reverberate in the air

Season word: *natsu no yama* (summer mountain; summer)

Misuzu took an overdose of sleeping pills on March 9, 1930 and died the next day.

Ishikoro (The Pebble)

It made the child fall yesterday.

It made the horse stumble today.

I wonder who will hit it tomorrow.

The pebble in the country road

seems indifferent

and stays put in the red sunset.[80]

緋のダリア

　　田舎の道の

　　　　石に咲く

Hi no daria

　　inaka no michi no

　　　　ishi ni saku

The red dahlia

　　blooms by the pebble

　　　　on the country road

Season word: *daria* (dahlia; summer)

Natsu (Summer)

"Summer" is a night owl.

It is a slug-a-bed.

"Summer" is still awake at night

after I go to bed.

But "summer" is not yet awake

when I wake up the morning glory

in the early morning.

The cool, cool breeze

is blowing.[81]

夏の朝

    そよ風起こす

        子と花よ

Natsu no asa

    soyo kaze okosu

        ko to hana yo

The summer morning

    the girl and the flower

        wake up the cool breeze

Season word: *natsu no asa* (summer morning; summer)

Natsu no yoi (Summer Evening)

Even after the sunset,

the color of the sky is light,

the star is playing the harmonica.

Even after the sunset,

the dust rises in the town,

the empty horse cart is clattering.

Even after the sunset,

the color of the soil is light,

the incense-stick firework is burning up.

The red fireball falls quietly.[82]

線香花火

    少女の願ひ

        闇と散る

Senkō hanabi

    shōjo no negai

        yami to chiru

Burning the incense-stick fireworks

    the girl's wishes

        disappeared in the darkness

Season word: *senkō hanabi* (incense-stick fireworks for children; summer)

Ryōshi no ojisan (Mr. Fisherman)

"Mr. Fisherman,

please let me ride on your boat."

"Please take me to the place,

where the pretty clouds over there

are rising from the sea."

"I will give you my doll,

the only doll I have.

I will also give you my goldfish."

"Mr. Fisherman,

please let me ride on your boat."[83]

金魚玉

　　大海に浮く

　　　　ブイのごと

Kingyo dama

　　taikai ni uku

　　　　bui no goto

The hanging goldfish bowl

　　is swinging in the wind

　　　　like the buoy floating on the ocean

Season word: *kingyo dama* (a small hanging glass bowl used to suspend goldfish under the eaves; summer)

Umi no o-miya: O-hanashi no uta 4 (Undersea Palace: Poems for Fairytales No. 4)

The Undersea Palace is made of blue jade.
It is a blue palace like the moonlit night.

In the blue palace
Princess Oto is watching the sea all day long,
thinking "When, when?"

No matter how long she watches,
Mr. Urashima,
Mr. Urashima,
who had returned to the land—.

The only things that are moving
in the kingdom of the sea in the quiet daytime are
the red sea plants
and their pale-purple shadows.

Even one hundred years later,
Princess Oto is still watching the sea,
thinking "When, when?"[84]

海亀や

　　大海原を

　　　　幾年も

Umi game ya

　　ō unabara o

　　　　ikutose mo

The sea turtle

　　has crossed the vast sea

　　　　for a hundred years

Season word: *umi game* (sea turtle; summer)
In the story of Urashima Tarō, a Japanese Rip Van Winkle, he went to the Undersea Palace, riding on the sea turtle he had rescued on the beach, and met Princess Oto there.

Sora no achira (Beyond the Sky)

What lies there

beyond the sky?

Neither thunder-and-lightning,

nor cumulonimbus cloud,

nor even the sun know.

Beyond the sky

lies the mysterious world

of magic,

where the mountain and the sea

talk to each other

and a person

is transformed into a crow.[85]

入道雲

　　夢見る少女

　　　　空青し

Nyūdo gumo

　　yume miru shōjo

　　　　sora aoshi

The cumulonimbus clouds

　　the girl is daydreaming

　　　　under the blue sky

Season word: *nyūdo gumo* (*nyūdō gumo*, cumulonimbus clouds; summer)

Ten'nin (The Celestial Muse)

As I watch alone the clouds
in the sunset glory
on the grass hill in the evening,

I remember the gentle eyebrows
of the celestial muse playing the flute,

riding on the pretty cloud
in the dark wooden panel
below the ceiling
at the temple I once visited.

Perhaps, my mother might also be
riding on such a pretty cloud,
dancing in a thin gown
and playing the flute now.

As I watch the clouds
in the sunset glory,
I somehow hear the sound of the flute,
the faint sound far away.[86]

朝焼や

　　天女の調べ

　　　　笛と琴

Asa yake ya

　　ten'nyo no shirabe

　　　　fue to koto

The sunrise glory

　　the song of the celestial muse

　　　　the sound of the lute and the flute

Season word: *asa yake* (sunrise glory; summer)
In Misuzu's poem, "the wooden panel" (ranma) refers to a space above the sliding doors in the traditional Japanese room, in which an openwork wooden relief carving is installed.

O-tsuki-san (The Moon)

The moon at dawn
is at the edge of the mountain.

The white parrot in the cage
glances at it, with sleepy eyes, and thinking
"Here comes my company. I shall call to it to come here."

The moon in the daytime
is at the bottom of the marsh.

The child at the shore, wearing a straw hat,
stares at it, holding his fishing pole, thinking
"It is nice. I shall catch it. I wonder if I can catch it."

The moon at dusk
is among the tree branches.

The little bird with a red beak
guards it, with wide open eyes, thinking
"It is very ripe. I shall peck at it."[87]

夏の月

　　みんなの願ひ

　　　　叶へたり

Natsu no tsuki

　　min'na no negai

　　　　kanae tari

The summer moon

　　grants

　　　　the wishes of everyone

Season word: *natsu no tsuki* (summer moon; summer)

Hiroi o-sora (The Wide Sky)

I wish I could go out to a place someday,

where I can see the wide, wide sky.

The sky I see in town is a long, narrow sky.

Even the Milky Way runs from roof to roof.

I wish I could go out

to the very end of the Milky Way

once someday,

where it meets the sea,

where I could see everything at a glance.[88]

天の川

    織姫の夢

        紡ぐ夜

Ama no gawa

    Orihime no yume

        tsumugu yoru

The Milky Way

    is weaving the dream

        of Princess Weaver at night

Season word: *ama no gawa* (Milky Way; autumn)
Princess Weaver (Vega) refers to a protagonist in a legend in which the princess and the Cowherd (Altair) can meet only once a year, on July 7 (in the old calendar), at the Milky Way. In haiku, August 7 marks the beginning of autumn.

Sora no ō-kawa (The Big River in the Sky)

On the riverbed in the sky,

many pebbles are lying,

swaying with each other.

On the blue river,

the crescent moon is sailing quietly,

like a slender white sail.

In the stream that runs like a dream,

the stars are floating,

like little boats made of reed blades.[89]

Japanese children used to make little boats out of reed blades and floated them on the river.

大星河

　　津波の里に

　　　　降り注ぐ

Dai seiga

　　tsunami no sato ni

　　　　furi sosogu

The Milky Way

　　shines over the villages

　　　　that were struck by the tsunami

Season word: *seiga* (Milky Way; autumn)

O-tsuki-sama no uta (The Song of the Moon)

"How old is the moon?"
"How old is the moon?"
    My nanny taught me the song
    under the evening moon just like this one.

"It is thirteen days and nine hours old."
"It is thirteen days and nine hours old."
    She is teaching the song to my younger brother now
    in the same backdoor, pulling his hands.

"It is still young."
"It is still young."
    I no longer sing it these days.
    I forgot it even when I saw the moon.

"How old is the moon?"
"How old is the moon?"
    An invisible nanny will pull my hands
    and make me remember it.[90]

This refers to a lullaby traditionally sung in the local dialect of Yamaguchi prefecture. "Nine hours" corresponds to around 12:00 noon in modern time counting.

待宵草

　　ひと月早き

　　　　月見なり

Matsu yoi gusa

　　hitotsuki hayaki

　　　　tsukimi nari

The evening primrose

　　is having a moon viewing party

　　　　a month early

Season word: *tsuki mi* (moon viewing party; autumn)

The evening primrose has moon-like yellow flowers. It blooms in summer as well as in autumn.

September

Photograph 9: Tray with the design of a rabbit in the moon.

Kyonen no kyō: Daishinsai kinenbi ni (Today A Year Ago: On the one-year memorial anniversary day of the Great Kantō Earthquake)

Today a year ago at this time,
I was playing with the blocks.
The block castle I had made crumbled loudly
and scattered away at once.

Today a year ago in the evening,
I was staying on the grass outside.
I was scared of the black fire,
but I saw my mother's eyes watching me.

Today a year ago after the evening,
thousands of houses were burned.
The dress that arrived on that day was burned,
so was the block castle I had made.

Today a year ago late at night,
I saw the shadow of the white moon,
among the clouds that were reflecting the color of the fire,
and saw my mother holding me tight.

My clothes are all new,
my new house is already built,
but my mother that day is gone.
This year is lonely.[91]

震災忌

　都鳥啼く

　　隅田川

Shinsai ki

　miyako dori naku

　　Sumida gawa

The memorial day of the Great Kantō Earthquake

　the black-headed gull cries

　　on the bank of the Sumida River

Season word: *Shinsai ki* (Memorial anniversary day of the Great Kantō Earthquake, September 1; autumn)
The Great Kantō Earthquake shook the Tokyo metropolitan region on September 1, 1923. Misuzu's younger brother lived in Tokyo at that time. It appears that Misuzu in this poem juxtaposed her childhood memory with the one-year anniversary of this tragic event. The Sumida River runs through Tokyo.

Aki wa ichiya ni (Autumn Comes in One Night)

Autumn comes in one night.

The wind blows
on the Two Hundred and Tenth Day.

The rain falls
on the Two Hundred and Twentieth Day.

If it stops at dawn the next day,
it sneaks in again at night that day.

No one knows
if it lands at the port by boat,
or if it flies in the sky with its wings,

or if it swells up from the earth,
but it is already here this morning.

No one knows where it is,
but it is already here somewhere.[92]

又三郎

    二百十日の

        風と消ゆ

Matasaburō

    Nihyaku tōka no

        kaze to kiyu

Matasaburō

    has disappeared in the wind

        of the Two Hundred and Tenth Day

Season word: *Nihyaku tōka* (The two hundred and tenth day from the arrival of spring on February 4; autumn) Matasaburō is a protagonist in Miazawa Kenji's *Kaze no Matasaburō* (Matasaburō the Wind). The "Two Hundred and Tenth Day" usually falls on September 1. It is a day of warning for farmers of the beginning of the typhoon season.

Aki (Autumn)

The electric light shines the way it wants to

and creates shadows the way it wants to,

making the town look like pretty stripes.

In the bright stripes,

there are several women,

wearing summer cotton yukatas.

In the dark stripes,

the autumn is

quietly hiding.[93]

蟲の音や

　　そぞろ歩きの

　　　　街の路地

Mushi no ne ya

　　sozoro aruki no

　　　　machi no roji

The insect chirps

　　in the back alley of the street

　　　　where people are strolling

Season word: *mushi no ne* (insect chirps; autumn)

Ō-tomari minato (Ō-tomari Seaport)

On the way back from the mountain festival,

when I departed with my aunt who saw me off
and climbed down the pass,

I saw the reflection of the beautiful sea
sparkling on the cedar branches.

On the sea, I saw the mast and the moored boat.
On the coast, I saw the thatched roofs here and there.

All seemed as if they were in the sky.
All seemed as if they were in the dream.

As I climbed down the pass,
I saw the buckwheat field.

At the end of the field,
I saw the same old Ō-tomari,

the old, lonely seaport.[94]

蕎麦の花

　真白き風を

　　揺らしたり

Soba no hana

　ma shiroki kaze o

　　yurashi tari

The buckwheat blossoms

　are gently swinging

　　in the pure white wind

Season word: *soba no hana* (buckwheat blossoms; autumn)
Buckwheat blossoms are pure white. In Misuzu's poem, Ō-tomari Seaport is on Ōmi Island, her father's birthplace, is one of the Eight Scenic Sites of Senzaki.

Tsuki no de (The Moonrise)

Be quiet, be quiet,

look,

it is rising.

The edge of the mountain

is vaguely light.

At the bottom of the sky

and at the bottom of the sea,

something shining

is melting.[95]

白き月

　　海の真珠を

　　　　あやしたり

Shiroki tsuki

　　umi no shinju o

　　　　ayashi tari

The white moon

　　is lulling

　　　　the baby pearls in the sea

Season word: *tsuki* (moon; autumn)

Mon tsuki (Formal Kimono with Family Crest)

The quiet autumn dusk

was wearing a pretty formal kimono with a family crest.

The moon is the white family crest.

The blue mountain is the pattern of the bottom of the

kimono, in a light-blue color of thinned indigo.

The glittering sea is the silver powder.

The flickering light on the blue mountain

is the brocade.

I wonder where it is going to be wed.

The quiet autumn dusk

was wearing a pretty formal kimono with a family crest.[96]

月今宵

　　金銀緞子の

　　　　花嫁よ

Tsuki koyoi

　　kin gin donsu no

　　　　hana yome yo

The moon tonight

　　is sending off the bride

　　　　wearing the gold and silver brocade kimono

Season word: *tsuki koyoi* (*lit.*, "the moon tonight" refers to the "mid-autumn full moon," the full moon of August in the old calendar, which falls around mid or late September today; autumn)

Tsuki to kumo (The Moon and the Clouds)

The moon and the clouds
accidentally met
in the middle of the field
in the sky.

The clouds were in a hurry
and cannot detour,
the moon too was in a hurry
and cannot stop.

Saying "Pardon me,"
the moon passed over
the clouds primly
and moved on.

Having their heads stepped on
by the moon,
the clouds moved on
nonchalantly.[97]

名月や

　　月の兎の

　　　　運動会

Mei getsu ya

　　tsuki no usagi

　　　　no undōkai

The fine full moon night

　　the rabbit on the moon

　　　　is having a field day

Season word: *mei getsu* (the mid-autumn full moon, the full moon on August 15 in the old calendar; autumn) Japanese legend has it that a rabbit lives on the moon pounding rice to make rice cakes.

Kaguyahime: O-hanashi no uta 2 (Princess Kaguya: Poems for Fairytales No. 2)

The princess who was born from the bamboo

has returned to the moon.

The princess who has returned to the moon

cried every moonlit night looking down on earth.

She cried missing her old home on earth,

she cried feeling sorry for the foolish people.

The princess cried every night without fail,

but the world down on earth has changed fast.

The old man and the old woman have died

and the foolish people have forgotten about her.[98]

望月や

　　御伽草子を

　　　　語る星

Mochi zuki ya

　　otogi zōshi o

　　　　kataru hoshi

The mid-autumn full moon

　　the star is reciting

　　　　the fairytale

Season word: *mochi zuki* (the mid-autumn full moon; autumn)

Isogashii sora (The Busy Sky)

The sky is busy tonight.

The clouds are running away fast
one after another.

They bump into the half moon
and yet they are running away
nonchalantly.

The little cloud is roaming around
and is in the way.
The big cloud is chasing after it.

Being tucked inside the clouds,
the half moon keeps moving
through the clouds.

The sky is busy tonight.
It is truly busy.[99]

The half moon refers to the first quarter moon.

芒の穂

　　月夜の雲を

　　　　追ひ払ふ

Susuki no ho

　　tsuki yo no kumo o

　　　　oi harau

The silver grass

　　is sweeping away

　　　　the clouds from the moon at night

Season words: *susuki* (silver grass; autumn) and *tsuki yo* (moonlit night; autumn)
Susuki (*miscanthus sinensis*) is one of the "seven plants of autumn."

Hiru no tsuki (The Moon in the Daytime)

The moon looks like a bubble.

If blown on,

it looks like it would disappear.

At this moment in a foreign country,

the traveler crossing a desert is saying

"It is dark. It is dark."

"White moon in the daytime,

why don't you go to him?"[100]

月明り

    キャラバン隊の

        道案内

Tsuki akari

    kyaraban tai no

        michi anai

The moonlight

    is guiding

        the caravan in the desert

Season word: *tsuki akari* (moonlight; autumn)

October

Photograph 10. Full moon with Mars (above the moon).

Tsuki no o-fune (The Moon Boat)

The sky is filled with sardine-like clouds.

The sea in the sky is swung by big waves.

The silver boat of Senmatsu,

who is returning from Sado Island,

appears and disappears.

Even with its golden oar having been swept away,

I wonder when the boat can sail home.

Appearing and disappearing,

the boat sails

from one end of the rough sea to the other.[101]

鰯雲

    漁師勇みて

        沖に出る

Iwashi gumo

    ryōshi isami te

        oki ni deru

The sardine clouds

    the fisherman is excited in anticipation

        of a big catch and sail to the sea

Season word: *iwashi gumo* (*lit.*, "sardine-like clouds," cirrocumulus clouds; autumn)
It has been said in fishing communities that cirrocumulus clouds bring a good catch of sardines.

Yofuke no sora (The Sky in the Late Night)

When people and plants are sleeping,

the sky is truly busy.

Every star is flying across the sky, twinkling,

each carrying a beautiful dream on its back,

in order to deliver to everyone's beds.

The dew princess is rushing the silver horse carriage,

in order to distribute the dew to everything before dawn,

to the flowers on the balcony in town,

and to the undergrowth deep in the mountain.

When flowers and children are sleeping,

the sky is truly busy.[102]

露草や

　　夜露をもらひ

　　　　青作る

Tsuyu kusa ya

　　yo tsuyu o morai

　　　　ao tsukuru

The dayflower

　　receives the night dew

　　　　and creates the color of blue

Season word: *tsuyu kusa* (*lit.*, "dew plant," Asiatic dayflower; autumn)
This dainty flower blooms only for one day and pops out its seeds. The plant self-sows and spreads rapidly; hence, it is regarded as a weed in eastern North America.

Tsuki no hikari (The Moonlight)

Part One

The moonlight peeks

at the brightly lit town

from the rooftop.

Without noticing it,

people walk in the town happily

as if it were daytime.

The moonlight watches them

and sighs quietly

and throws away on the rooftiles

many shadows that no one would want.

Without even noticing it,

people pass through the brightly lit street

like fish swim through the stream,

      dragging the fickle shadow of the electric light

      that becomes dark and light at each step

      and stretches and shrinks at each step.

Part Two

The moonlight finds

the dark, lonely back alley.

It quickly dives into it.

It dives into the eyes

of the poor orphan,

when she was surprised

and raises her eyes.

Without hurting her eyes at all,

it makes the shack there

look like a silver palace.

The child eventually falls asleep,

but the moonlight stays there

quietly until dawn,

      giving constant shadows

      to the broken horse cart,

      the broken umbrella,

      and even a single grass blade.[103]

十六夜や

　　月光菩薩の

　　　　使者となり

Izayoi ya

　　Gekkō bosatsu no

　　　　shisha to nari

The sixteenth-night moon

　　has become the messenger of

　　　　the Moonlight Goddess of Mercy

Season word: *izayoi* (the sixteenth-night moon in August in the old calendar; autumn)
The Moonlight Goddess of Mercy is one of a pair of guardians of Buddha, along with the Sunlight Goddess of Mercy.

Yamiyo no hoshi (The Star in the Dark Night)

In the dark night

there is a lost star.

Is it a girl?

The star is alone

like me.

Is it a girl?[104]

ペガサスや

　　迷子の星を

　　　　乗せ飛翔

Pegasasu ya

　　maigo no hoshi o

　　　　nose hishō

Pegasus

　　carried the little lost star on its back

　　　　and flew away

Season word: *Pegasasu* (constellation Pegasus; autumn)

Hoshi no kazu (The Number of the Stars)

With only ten fingers,

I have been counting

the number of the stars,

yesterday and today.

With only ten fingers,

I shall keep counting

the number of the stars,

forever and ever.[105]

星月夜

　　ゴッホの夢を

　　　　描きたり

Hoshi zuki yo

　　Gohho no yume o

　　　　egaki tari

The starry night

　　has drawn

　　　　the dream of van Gogh

Season word: *hoshi zuki yo* (starry night as bright as a moonlit night; autumn)

"van Gogh" refers to Vincent van Gogh (1853–1890).

Mienai hoshi (The Invisible Stars)

What is beyond the sky?

There are stars beyond the sky.
What is beyond the stars?

There are also stars beyond the stars.
There are stars that we cannot see.

What are the stars that we cannot see?

They are the soul of the king
who had many attendants.
It wants to be alone.

And the soul of the dancer
who was watched by many people.
It wants to hide.[106]

カシオペア

    星のワルツの

        振付師

Kashiopea

    hoshi no warutsu no

        furitsuie shi

Cassiopeia

    is choreographing

        the "waltz of the stars"

Season word: *Kashiopea* (constellation Cassiopeia; autumn)

Queen Cassiopeia is a protagonist in Greek mythology.

Mizu to kaze to kodomo (The Water, the Wind, and the Child)

What circles

around heaven and earth?

It is water.

What circles

around the world?

It is wind.

What circles

around the persimmon tree?

It is the child

who wants its fruit.[107]

柿熟れる

　　子の寝るうちに

　　　　鳥の啄む

Kaki ureru

　　ko no neru uchi ni

　　　　tori no tsui bamu

The persimmons ripened

　　the birds ate them all

　　　　before the child woke up in the morning

Season word: *kaki* (persimmon; autumn)

Gion-sha (Gion Shrine)

With the pine needles gently falling,

the shrine in autumn feels lonely.

Ah, the peeking song, the gaslight, and

the cinnamon tree wearing a red sash.

Only the autumn wind is swishing

on the abandoned ice shop.[108]

Gion Shrine (current Yasaka Shrine) in Senzaki is one of the Eight Scenic Sites of Senzaki. "Gion" might stand for Zion, as the resemblances between the rituals of the Gion shrines (its head shrine is Yasaka Shrine in Kyoto, known for the Gion Festival), and those of Hebrew shrines have been noted recently.

棗の実

　　森の社の

　　　　鈴の鳴る

Natsume no mi

　　mori no yashiro no

　　　　suzu no naru

The jujubes

　　the bells are ringing

　　　　at the shrine in the woods

Season word: *natsume no mi* (jujubes; autumn)

Jujubes are fruits originating in the Middle East.

Arashi no yoru (The Night of the Storm)

The howling wind,
the raging waves.

At the shore
the lighthouse keeper
is talking to himself.

"I wonder if
the pearls are still there,
in and at the bottom."

The swirling wind,
the swirling clouds.

Above them
the blue star
is talking to itself.

"I wonder if
the buds of last night will bloom there,
in and at the bottom."[109]

野分立つ

　　光琳

　　　　宗達に学ぶ

Nowaki tatsu

　　Kōrin

　　　　Sōtatsu ni manabu

The typhoon struck

　　Kōrin

　　　　keeps studying Sōtatsu

Season word: *nowaki* (typhoon; autumn)
Kōrin refers to Ogata Kōrin (1658–1716), who painted folding screens, including the "Irises Screen" (a National Treasure of Japan). He studied and copied the painting of the "Wind God and Thunder God" by Tawaraya Sōtatsu (?–circa 1640).

Jūsanya (The Thirteenth-night Moon)

The shower that fell this morning

had snow pellets mixed in.

Suddenly,

the cold wind began to blow yesterday

and my mother put the new paper screen

on the sliding door.

Now,

even the clouds have disappeared

and the moon shines clear and cold.

Suddenly,

the insects that chirp in this grass field

have become scarce.[110]

Snow pellets (*arare*) are smaller than hailstones (*hyō*).

十三夜

    傾げる顔の

        いとおかし

Jūsanya

    kashigeru kao no

        ito okashi

The Thirteenth-night Moon

    its slightly tilted face

        has its own beauty

Season word: Jūsanya (the Thirteenth-night Moon; autumn)

Jūsanya refers to the moon on September 13 in the old calendar, which falls in mid or late October today. The Fifteenth-night Moon (on August 15 in the old calendar) and the Thirteenth-night Moon, as a pair, are regarded as the best moons of the year.

November

Photograph 11. Dandelion puff ball.

Hoshi to tanpopo (The Star and the Dandelion)

Deep in the blue sky,

like the pebbles in the sea,

the stars lie at the bottom until night comes.

The stars in the daytime are invisible.

>They are invisible, but they exist.

>Invisible things do exist.

Deep in the rooftile,

the fallen, withered dandelions lie quietly.

They hide until the spring comes.

Their strong roots are invisible.

>They are invisible, but they exist.

>Invisible things do exist.[111]

枯れし蒲公英

　流れし星と

　　雲となり

Kareshi tanpopo

　nagareshi hoshi to

　　kumo to nari

The dead dandelion

　the shooting star turned it

　　into the cloud

Season word: *nagareshi hoshi* (*nagare boshi*, shooting star; autumn)

Funanori to hoshi (The Sailor and the Star)

The sailor looked at the star.

The star said, "Come to me. Come to me."

The waves were very high.

The sailor's eyes shone with excitement.

Without fearing the wind or looking at the waves,

he headed the bow of his boat toward the star.

Without his knowing, the sailor landed on the shore.

He thought, "This is the star! This is the star!"

But the star was far away after all.

Having missed catching the sailor,

the waves became angrier.[112]

碇星

    彷徨ふ漁師

        天に乞ふ

Ikari boshi

    samayou ryōshi

        ten ni kou

Cassiopeia

    the lost fisherman

        prays to the heavens

Season word: *Ikari boshi* (*lit.*, "anchor star" refers to constellation Cassiopeia; autumn)
"Ikari boshi" is an archaic Japanese name for the constellation Cassiopeia. Japanese fishermen associated the shape of the constellation with an anchor.

Tōi kaji (The Fire Far Away)

The fire far away,
as if, having forgotten about it,
we were playing war.

"Extinguished, extinguished,"
one came running and saying.

Under someone's nose,
a combat technician seized
a landmine of the enemy.

After the battle was over,
as we were panting on the roadside,
the third team withdrew.

It passed by blowing the trumpet.
We saw them off quietly.

In the sky
where the [fire] pump was moving black,
the half moon was carrying a huge umbrella.[113]

The half moon refers to the first quarter moon.

冬夕焼

    トランペットの

        音遥か

Fuyu yuyake

    toranpetto no

        oto haruka

The winter sunset glow

    the sound of the trumpet

        reverberates far away

Season word: *fuyu yuyake* (winter sunset glow; winter)

In haiku, November 7 marks the beginning of winter.

Gakkō e yuku michi (The Way to the School)

The way to school is long,
so I always think of stories.

If I do not encounter anyone on the way,
I keep thinking of stories
until I arrive at the school.

But if I encounter someone,
I would have to say morning greetings.

Then, I would remember
about the weather, the frost,
and the lonely rice paddies.

Therefore, I would rather not
encounter anyone on the way,

and pass the school gate
before my stories end.[114]

霜柱

　　耕馬の蹄

　　　　しづしづと

Shimo bashira

　　kōba no hizume

　　　　shizu shizu to

The needle ice

　　the hooves of the plow horse

　　　　are stepping on the field slowly

Season word: *shimo bashira* (*lit.*, "frost pillar," needle ice; winter)
For reference, there is a season word, 'mugi fumi' (stepping on a wheatfield), which signifies spring.

Minato no yoru (The Night at the Seaport)

It is a cloudy night.

A little star is shivering.

One.

It is a cold night.

The light on the boat

is reflected and swaying.

Two.

It is a lonely night.

The eye of the sea

is shining blue.

Three.[115]

凍星や

　　異国に泊まる

　　　　船照らす

Ite boshi ya

　　ikoku ni tomaru

　　　　fune teraru

The freezing star

　　is shining on the ship

　　　　harbored in a foreign country

Season word: *ite boshi* (freezing star; winter)

Kita kaze no uta (The Song of the North Wind)

When the sound of the wintry wind
in the middle sky stopped suddenly,
I thought—.

The wind in the middle sky said,
"Listen to the song,
listen to my song."

"The song of the bird
that lives on the ice field,
the bell of the sleigh
that runs in the open snow field,
I brought them all—."

With no one answering,
with no one listening,
the wind in the middle sky
felt lonely suddenly—.[116]

忘れ花

    風に晒され

        誰を待つ

Wasure bana

    kaze ni sarasare

        dare o matsu

The forgotten flower

    whom is it waiting for

        trembling in the winter wind

Season word: *wasure bana* (*lit.*, "forgotten flower" refers to flower unseasonably blooming in winter; winter)

Hatsu arare (The First Snow Pellets of the Season)

Snow pellets, snow pellets.

As I catch them in my hands,
I suddenly think of the Hina Doll Festival
on the spring night.

On a night like this,
the dear old Hina dolls of my neighbor
must be staying in a box for each one
in the dark corner of the warehouse.

They must be listening
to the sound of the snow pellets
hitting the gutter intermittently.

Snow pellets, snow pellets,
the first snow pellets of the season.[117]

初霰

　若き詩人の

　　顕わるる

Hatsu arare

　wakaki shijin no

　　arawaruru

The first snow pellets

　the young poet

　　was born

Season word: *hatsu arare* (the first snow pellets of the season; winter)

In Misuzu's poem, she associated the snow pellets (*arare*) with the Hina Doll Festival, because children eat *hina arare* (colorful rice cracker pellets) for the festival on March 3.

Fuyu no hoshi (The Star in the Winter)

In the town

in the frosty night,

my elder sister said,

watching the sky,

      —"Good-bye"

          quietly and cold.

Star in the sky

in the frosty night,

the bluest star

in the sky,

      —It was as if

         saying to you.[118]

霜降る夜

　　上りの汽笛

　　　　霞みゆく

Shimo furu yo

　　nobori no kiteki

　　　　kasumi yuku

The frosty night

　　the whistling of the train bound for Tokyo

　　　　is getting faint

Season word: *shimo furu* ("frost falls"; winter)

Mise no dekigoto (A Thing Happened at the Store)

The snow pellets entered the store
through the small side door.

The customer entered the store
along with the snow pellets.

> "Good evening."
> "Welcome to the store."

The music-box clock [uta dokei] rang
in the hand of the customer.
Mixed with the sound of the snow pellets
it sang a children's counting rhyme.

> "Good-bye."
> "Thank you for your patronage."

The music-box clock left the store, ringing.

As I listened to the sound until it stopped,
the snow pellets had already stopped
when I suddenly noticed.[119]

霰降る

　　主人慌てて

　　　　盆栽入れる

Arare furu

　　aruji awatete

　　　　bonsai ireru

The snow pellets are falling

　　the master of the house

　　　　takes the bonsai pots inside in a hurry

Season word: *arare* (snow pellets; winter)

Snow pellets (*arare*) are smaller than hailstones (*hyō*).

An'ya (The Dark Night)

In the dark open field

someone is singing

a song for schoolchildren.

A shadow is cast

on one of the window lights

arrayed on the hill.

The sky over the big city far away

is obscuring the gold dust

faintly.

Being alone on the laundry-drying balcony,

I keep watching the sky

eating a mandarin orange.[120]

寂しき娘

　　蜜柑畑の

　　　　見果てぬ夢よ

Samishiki ko

　　mikan batake no

　　　　mihatenu yume yo

The lonely girl

　　keeps dreaming

　　　　of the mandarin orange grove

Season word: *mikan batake* (mandarin orange grove; winter)

December

Photograph 12. Kadomatsu decoration for the new year, under Creative Commons license, "Pair gate with [bamboo and] pine branches for the new year, kadomatsu, Katori-city, Japan," January 2, 2007, https://commons.wikimedia.org/wiki/File:Pair_gate_with_pine_branches_for_the_New_Year,kadomatsu,katori-city,japan.JPGWinter sky.

Kumo II (The Cloud II)

Looking for someone on the mountain,

the cloud descended onto it.

Finding no one on the mountain,

the cloud came away from it.

Looking disappointed,

the cloud flew away,

in the evening sky

alone.[121]

白き山

　　鉛の空に

　　　　鷹一羽

Shiroki yama

　　namari no sora ni

　　　　taka ichi wa

The white mountain

　　the hawk is flying alone

　　　　in the lead-like sky

Season word: *taka* (hawk; winter)

Kumo no kodomo (The Child Cloud)

The child wave plays

where there is the child wind.

The adult wind is also there

where there is the adult wave.

But I feel sorry for the child cloud

that is traveling in the sky.

Because it is accompanied

by the adult wind

and is following it

breathlessly.[122]

北の空

　　親鳥を追ふ

　　　　若き鷲

Kita no sora

　　oya dori o ou

　　　　wakaki washi

The northern sky

　　the juvenile eagle

　　　　is soaring with its parent

Season word: *washi* (eagle; winter)

Yuki ni (Asking the Snow)

The snow that falls on the sea

becomes the sea.

The snow that falls on the town

becomes a mudpuddle.

The snow that falls on the mountain

remains snow.

The snow that is still in the sky,

which one would you like to become?[123]

スノー・グローブ

　　故郷探る

　　　　下関の娘

Sunō grōbu

　　furusato saguru

　　　　Shimonoseki no ko

The snow globe

　　the girl in Shimonoseki

　　　　is searching for her hometown

Season word: *sunō grōbu* (snow globe; winter)

Kona yuki (The Powder Snow)

"Powder snow,

powder snow,

you are too white."

"Powder snow,

fall on the pine tree,

and be dyed in green."[124]

雪吊や

　　老松背筋

　　　　伸したり

Yuki tsuiri ya

　　oi matsu sesuji

　　　　nobashi tari

The 'snow hangings' having been put on

　　the old pine

　　　　stretches its back

Season word: *yuki tsuiri* (*lit.*, "to hang snow," a device to protect trees from heavy snow; winter)
"Yuki tsuiri" refers to a tradition to install structures made of ropes around tree—like umbrella spines—so that snow will not accumulate on the branches. Kenroku Garden in Kanazawa, Ishikawa prefecture, is famous for this serene winter scene.

Tsumotta yuki (The Snow Pile)

The snow on top
must feel cold.

For it is exposed
to the chilly, piercing moon.

The snow at the bottom
must feel weighed down.

For it carries
hundreds of people on top of it.

The snow in the middle
must feel lonely.

For it can see
neither the sky nor the earth.[125]

冬薔薇

    雪に眠りし

        淋しき王女

Fuyu sōbi

    yuki ni nemurishi

        sabishiki ōjo

The winter rose

    the lonely princess

        sleeps under the snow

Season words: *fuyu sōbi* (winter rose; winter) and *yuki* (snow; winter)

Garasu (The Window Glass)

I remember the window glass

that fell and broke into pieces

on the ground on a snowy day.

I kept thinking about the window glass pieces

that I shall pick them up later

but kept procrastinating.

I kept thinking about the window glass pieces

whenever I saw a dog limping

that the dog might have had walked on them that day.

I cannot forget the window glass pieces

that was shining on the snow

on the snowy day.[126]

大雪原

 樺太犬の

  橇の往く

Dai setsu gen

 Karafuto inu no

  sori no yuku

The vast snow field

 the Sakhalin Huskies

  are pulling the sleigh at a run

Season words: *setsu gen* (snow field; winter) and *sori* (sleigh; winter)

The ill-fated Sakhalin Huskies, used for the Japanese expeditions to Antarctica, were featured in the films *Nankyoku Monogatari* (A Tale of Antarctica, 1983) and *Eight Below* (2006).

Garasu no naka (Inside the Glass)

The snow was falling in front of the house
and it looked as if flower petals were falling,

so I was watching the glass picture
on the sliding door,
sitting under the kotatsu heater.

Then, I saw the shadow
of my grandmother's back

—walking in the falling snow
to fetch a log from the rear wooden hut—

flickering and then disappearing.[127]

This paper "sliding door" refers to an "akari shoji," part of which is made of glass, so that it admits light. Also, "yukimi shōji" is a snow-viewing sliding door, whose lower part is made of glass so that people can watch the snow falling, while sitting in a room.

吹雪の夜

　門を叩くは

　　雪女やも

Fubuki no yo

　mon o tataku wa

　　yuki on'na yamo

The night of the blizzard

　could the woman who is knocking on the door

　　be the snow woman?

Season words: *fubuki* (blizzard; winter) and *yuki on'na* (snow woman; winter)

Yuki on'na is an imaginary creature in Japanese folklore.

Fuyu no ame (The Rain in Winter)

"Mother, mother, look for a moment.
Snow is falling mixed with rain."

My mother said, "Yes, it is."
My mother is sewing a kimono.

> —People walk in the street in the sleet,
>   carrying umbrellas that all look similar.

"Mother, if I slept seven more nights,
will New Year's Day come for sure?"

My mother said, "Yes, it will."
My mother is sewing a spring kimono.

> —I wish this mudpuddle were a river.
>   It would be even better if it were a big sea.

"Mother, a boat is passing,
with the oar making a squeaking sound."

Mother said, "You are silly."
My mother does not look toward me.

> —Feeling lonely I put my left cheek on the window.
>   The glass was very cold.[128]

数へ日を

　　数へて偲ぶ

　　　　我が祖国

Kazoe bi o

　　kazoe te shinobu

　　　　waga sokoku

Counting the days until New Year's Day

　　while reminiscing

　　　　about one's home country

Season word: *kazoe bi* (counting the days until New Year's Day; winter)

O-shōgatsu to tsuki (New Year's Day and the Moon)

Moon,

why are you getting thin?

Why are you getting thin

like the pine needles

of the kadomatsu ornament?

At a time

when New Year's Day

is coming.[129]

Kadomatsu (*lit.*, "pine gate") refers to New Year ornaments made of pine needles and bamboo leaves and trunks, placed in pairs in front of the gate, an equivalent to Christmas wreaths in the West.

門松立てる

　　下弦の月を

　　　　見上ぐる娘

Kadomatsu tateru

　　kagen no tsuki o

　　　　miaguru ko

Having erected the pine ornaments

　　the girl looks

　　　　at the thin waning moon

Season word: *kadomatsu tateru* (to erect pine ornaments at the gate for the New Year; signifies yearend)
"Kagen no tsuki" is the third (last) quarter moon, but in this haiku, it refers to a thinner waning moon, as in Misuzu's poem.

Ō-misoka to ganjitsu (New Year's Eve and New Year's Day)

My brother is going around collecting for bills.
My mother is decorating the house for New Year's Day.
I am delivering yearend thank-you gifts to customers.

Everyone in town is in a hurry.
The sun shines all over the town
and the whole town is somehow shining.

Above the pale-blue sky,
the black kite [bird] was drawing a circle quietly.

My brother is wearing a formal kimono.
My mother is also wearing a best kimono.
I too am wearing a long-sleeved kimono.

Everyone in town is playing.
The pine decorations are erected all over the town
and snow pellets are scattered all over the town.

Above the pale-gray sky,
the black kite was drawing a big circle.[130]

門松や

　　青き薫りの

　　　　空に満つ

Kadomatsu ya

　　aoki kaori no

　　　　sora ni mitsu

The pine ornaments

　　the scent of the fresh green

　　　　fills the air

Season word: *kadomatsu* (pine ornaments at the gate for the New Year; new year)

Notes

[1] Kaneko Misuzu, *Kaneko Misuzu zenshū* (Complete Works of Kaneko Misuzu), Tokyo: JULA shuppan-kyoku, 1984, Vol. 1, 116-117.

[2] Ibid., 61.

[3] Kaneko (1984), Vol. 2, 233-235.

[4] Ibid., 110-111.

[5] Kaneko (1984), Vol. 3, 108-109.

[6] Ibid., 151-152.

[7] Kaneko (1984), Vol. 2, 268.

[8] Ibid., 31-32. Misuzu wrote two poems with the same title "Hanabi (The Fireworks)." This book labels this poem as "Hanabi II" and another in Vol. 1 as "Hanabi I."

[9] Ibid., 191-192.

[10] Kaneko (1984), Vol. 3, 242.

[11] Ibid., 248-249. Misuzu wrote two poems with the same title "Gakkō (The School)." This book labels this poem as

"Gakkō II" and another in Vol. 2 as "Gakkō I."

[12] Kaneko (1984), Vol. 2, 173-174.

[13] Ibid., 122-123.

[14] Ibid., 23.

[15] Ibid., 223.

[16] Ibid., 45-46; Kaneko Misuzu, *Kaneko Misuzu dōyō-shū: Mayu to haka* (Anthology of Kaneko Misuzu's Poems: Cocoon and Grave), Danjō Harukiyo, ed., Tokyo: Kisetsu no mado shisha, 1970 (reprint, Tokyo: Ōzorasha, 1996), 23; originally published in *Dōwa*, February 1925, and then in *Aishō*, August 1928.

[17] Kaneko (1984), Vol. 2, 67.

[18] Kaneko (1984), Vol. 3, 251.

[19] Ibid., 181-182.

[20] Kaneko (1984), Vol. 2, 76.

[21] Kaneko (1984), Vol. 3, 177-178.

[22] Ibid., 179-180.

[23] Ibid., 250.

[24] Kaneko (1984), Vol. 1, 169-170; originally published in *Dōwa*, April 1926, and then in *Shokudai*, November 1928.

[25] Ibid., 44-45.

[26] Ibid., 43, originally published in *Fujin kurabu*, November 1923.

[27] Kaneko (1984), Vol. 3, 183-184.

[28] Ibid., 186-187.

[29] Kaneko (1984), Vol. 1, 189.

[30] Ibid., 223. Misuzu wrote two poems with the same title "Ho (The Sail)." This book labels this poem as "Ho I" and another in Vol. 3 as "Ho II."

[31] Kaneko (1984), Vol. 2, 39-40.

[32] Ibid., 267.

[33] Kaneko (1984), Vol. 3, 91-92; originally published in *Aishō*, February 1929.

[34] Kaneko (1984), Vol. 1, 226.

[35] Kaneko (1984), Vol. 2, 84.

[36] Kaneko (1970), 32; Kaneko (1984), Vol. 2, 129;

originally published in *Dōwa*, April 1926.

[37] Kaneko (1984), Vol. 2, 266.

[38] Ibid., 155-156.

[39] Kaneko (1984), Vol. 1, 82.

[40] Ibid.,74.

[41] Kaneko (1984), Vol. 2, 30.

[42] Ibid., 48-49.

[43] Kaneko (1984), Vol. 1, 143-144.

[44] Kaneko (1984), Vol. 2, 212-213. Misuzu wrote two poems with the same title "Gakkō (The School)." This book labels this poem as "Gakkō I" and another in Vol. 3 as "Gakkō II."

[45] Kaneko (1984), Vol. 3, 148.

[46] Kaneko (1984), Vol. 1, 118-119.

[47] Kaneko (1984), Vol. 2, 61.

[48] Kaneko (1984), Vol. 3, 162.

[49] Kaneko (1984), Vol. 2, 247-248.

[50] Kaneko (1984), Vol. 1, 213-214.

[51] Ibid., 85.

[52] Ibid., 69; originally published in *Dōwa*, January 1924.

[53] Kaneko (1984), Vol. 2, 94.

[54] Kaneko (1984), Vol. 3, 226. Misuzu wrote two poems with the same title "Kuregata (Dusk)." This book labels this poem as "Kuregata II" and another in Vol. 1 as "Kuregata I."

[55] Kaneko (1984), Vol. 2, 68.

[56] Ibid., 200.

[57] Kaneko (1984), Vol. 3, 67.

[58] Ibid., 223.

[59] Kaneko (1984), Vol. 2, 113-114.

[60] Kaneko (1984), Vol. 1, 51.

[61] Kaneko (1984), Vol. 3, 79-80.

[62] Ibid., 117.

[63] Ibid., 167.

[64] Kaneko (1984), Vol. 1, 168.

[65] Ibid., 192.

[66] Kaneko (1984), Vol. 3, 70-71.

[67] Kaneko (1984), Vol. 2, 65-66.

[68] Kaneko (1984), Vol. 1, 157-158.

[69] Ibid., 89.

[70] Ibid., 188.

[71] Kaneko (1984), Vol. 2, 50.

[72] Kaneko (1984), Vol. 1, 62.

[73] Kaneko (1970), 34; Kaneko (1984), Vol. 2, 60; originally published in *Dōwa*, June 1926.

[74] Kaneko (1984), Vol. 3, 234.

[75] Kaneko (1984), Vol. 1, 6-7. Misuzu wrote two poems with the same title "Kumo (The Cloud)." This book labels this poem as "Kumo I" and another in Vol. 2 as "Kumo II."

[76] Ibid., 234.

[77] Ibid., 229.

[78] Kaneko (1970), 21; Kaneko (1984), Vol. 1, 224; originally published in *Dōwa*, October 1924.

[79] Kaneko (1984), Vol. 3, 237-238.

[80] Kaneko (1984), Vol. 1, 134.

[81] Kaneko (1984), Vol. 3, 18.

[82] Ibid., 22-23.

[83] Kaneko (1984), Vol. 1, 95.

[84] Ibid., 20-21.

[85] Ibid., 11.

[86] Ibid., 124.

[87] Kaneko (1984), Vol. 3, 96-97.

[88] Kaneko (1984), Vol. 2, 51.

[89] Ibid., 9.

[90] Ibid., 12-13.

[91] Ibid., 26-27.

[92] Kaneko (1984), Vol. 3, 55.

[93] Kaneko (1984), Vol. 2, 38.

[94] Kaneko (1984), Vol. 3, 188.

[95] Kaneko (1984), Vol. 1, 136.

[96] Ibid., 65.

[97] Ibid., 28 29.

[98] Ibid.,16-17.

[99] Ibid.,76.

[100] Ibid.,106-107.

[101] Ibid., 112.

[102] Kaneko (1984), Vol. 2, 14.

[103] Ibid., 146-148.

[104] Ibid., 47.

[105] Ibid., 171-172.

[106] Kaneko (1984), Vol. 3, 15.

[107] Kaneko (1984), Vol. 2, 131.

[108] Kaneko (1984), Vol. 3, 189.

[109] Kaneko (1984), Vol. 2, 158-159.

[110] Kaneko (1984), Vol. 3, 199.

[111] Kaneko (1984), Vol. 2, 108.

[112] Ibid., 139-140.

[113] Kaneko (1984), Vol. 3, 72-73.

[114] Kaneko (1984), Vol. 2, 124-125.

[115] Ibid., 54.

[116] Ibid., 144-145.

[117] Kaneko (1984), Vol. 3, 98.

[118] Ibid., 100-101.

[119] Ibid., 104-105.

[120] Ibid., 257.

[121] Kaneko (1984), Vol. 2, 86. Misuzu wrote two poems with the same title "Kumo (The Cloud)." This book labels this poem as "Kumo II" and another in Vol. 1 as "Kumo I."

[122] Ibid., 132.

[123] Kaneko (1984), Vol. 3, 203.

[124] Kaneko (1984), Vol. 1, 159.

[125] Kaneko (1984), Vol. 2, 242.

[126] Kaneko (1970), 14; Kaneko (1984), Vol. 1, 133; originally published in *Dōwa*, May 1924.

[127] Kaneko (1984), Vol. 3, 110.

[128] Ibid., 274-275.

[129] Kaneko (1984), Vol. 1, 102.

[130] Kaneko (1984), Vol. 3, 106-107.

Selected Bibliography

"Akane no Kaneko Misuzu no tabi: Shi" (World of Kaneko Misuzu by Akane: Poems). July 28, 2017, http://akane.world.coocan.jp/misuzu/memorial/new-reference-18.htm.

Kaneko, Misuzu. *Kaneko Misuzu dōyō-shū: Mayu to haka* (Anthology of Kaneko Misuzu's Poems: Cocoon and Grave). Danjō Harukiyo, ed., Tokyo: Kisetsu no mado shisha, 1970; reprint, Tokyo: Ōzorasha, 1996.

Kaneko, Misuzu. *Kaneko Misuzu zenshū* (Complete Works of Kaneko Misuzu). 3 vols., Tokyo: JULA shuppan-kyoku, 1984.

Kaneko, Misuzu. *Something Nice.* Translated by D. P. Dutcher, Tokyo: Japan University Library Association, 1999; JULA shuppan-kyoku, 2001.

Kaneko, Misuzu. *Are You an Echo?: The Lost Poetry of*

Misuzu Kaneko. Illustrated by Toshikado Hajiri, translated by Sally Ito and Michiko Tsuboi, and text by David Jacobson, Seattle, WA: Chin Music Press, 2016.

"Kaneko Misuzu kinenkan: Kinenkan shokuin no nikki" (Kaneko Misuzu Memorial Museum: Staff Member's Diary). Periodically uploaded, https://www.city.nagato.yamaguchi.jp/site/misuzu/20073.html

"Kaneko Misuzu kinenkan: Yazaki Setsuo kanchō koramu" (Kaneko Misuzu Memorial Museum: Director Yazaki Setsuo's Column). Periodically uploaded, https://www.city.nagato.yamaguchi.jp/site/misuzu/34041.html.

"Kokoro no ōkoku: Dōyō shijin Kaneko Misuzu no sekai" (Kingdom of the Heart: World of Dōyō Poet Kaneko Misuzu). NHK Special, No. 853, August 27, 1995, uploaded February 18, 2017, https://www.

youtube.com/watch?v=CEpNNDjl_SE.

Kon'no, Tsutomu. *Kaneko Misuzu futatabi* (Revisiting Kaneko Misuzu). Tokyo: Shōgakukan, 1997, pbk., 2011.

Yazaki, Setsuo. *Misuzu Nōto* (Notes on Misuzu). Supplement to Kaneko Misuzu, *Kaneko Misuzu zenshū* (Complete Works of Kaneko Misuzu), 3 vols., Tokyo: JULA shuppan-kyoku, 1984.

_____. *Dōyō-shijin Kaneko Misuzu no shōgai* (Life of the Dōyō Poet Kaneko Misuzu). Tokyo: JULA shuppan-kyoku, 1993.

_____. *Kaneko Misuzu: Inochi to kokoro no uchū* (Kaneko Misuzu: Life and the Universe of Her Heart). Tokyo: JULA shuppan-kyoku, 2005.

_____. ed. *Botsugo 80-nen Kaneko Misuzu: Min'na chigatte min'na ii* (80-year Anniversary of Kaneko Misuzu's Death: All Are Different, All Are Good). Tokyo: JULA shuppan-kyoku, 2010.

About the Author

Mayumi Itoh is a former Professor of Political Science at the University of Nevada, Las Vegas. She has previously taught at Princeton University and Queens College, City University of New York, and has written many academic articles and books. Her book titles include: *Globalization of Japan: Japanese Sakoku Mentality and U.S. Efforts to Open Japan* (1998); *The Hatoyama Dynasty: Japanese Political Leadership Through the Generations* (2003); *Japanese War Orphans in Manchuria: Forgotten Victims of World War II* (2010); *Japanese Wartime Zoo Policy: The Silent Victims of World War II* (2010); *The Origin of Ping-Pong Diplomacy: The Forgotten Architect of Sino-U.S. Rapprochement* (2011); *Pioneers of Sino-Japanese Relations* (2012); *The Origins of Contemporary Sino-Japanese Relations: Zhou Enlai and Japan* (2016); *The Making of China's War with Japan* (2016); *The Making of China's Peace with Japan* (2017); *Hachiko* (2017); *Kaneko Misuzu: Life and Poems of A Lonely Princess* (2018); *The Japanese Culture of Mourning Whales* (2018); *Animals and the Fukushima Nuclear Disaster* (2018); *Haikus of All Seasons*, Vol. I–Vol. XI (2018–2019).

Made in United States
North Haven, CT
17 September 2023